Tales From
a Mid-Century Boy

Growing Up in Michigan

Kurt Struble

ISBN 978-1-954896-15-4 Hardbound
ISBN 978-1-954896-11-6 Paperback
ISBN 978-1-954896-12-3 ebook
Library of Congress Control Number: 2022912999

Image Credits:
Photographs by author
Michigan map by iStock.com/gio_banfi
Frog image by mvaligursky/Depositphotos.com
Oak tree image by doctor25/Depositphotos.com

1950schildhood.wordpress.com
FathomPublishing.com
Fathom Publishing Company
PO Box 200448 | Anchorage, AK 99520

Printed in the United States of America.

Dedication

This Book Is For
Dad
Who Gave His All

And
Laura Masters
John Struble
Matt Logan
Rebekah Logan
Khloe Logan
Max Oquendo
Louis Masters
Ben Masters
Heidi Oquendo
Christopher Oquendo

and of course,
Jodi Struble

To the faithful: Don Austin, Karen Karhoff Lewis, Barbara Karhoff, Don and Lynn Karhoff, Margaret Smith, Brenda Ryker, Janice Harper, John McKinnis, Bill Ramsey, Rick Middleton, Dottie Adams, Annie McAlpine, Rebecca McAlpine, Ron Anderson, Ron Chrzan, Rick Stone, Kay O'Neil, Kris Ballenger, Joan Sprague, Jo and Bill Rinker, Paul Spagnuolo, Pam Bruggeman Wells, Jeanne Plashek Newman, Lenore Chernenko, Candyce Y MW, Minde Renae, Susie Weinrich, Faith Barrs, Robert Sager, Diane Dimkoff, Carol Stroub, Merlin Parlett, Debbra Russell, Cheri Bogan, the thirty lives I was privileged to have touched from 1969–1970, and Nancy Streeter.

Lake Huron Shoreline
Late Winter Thaw

Contents

Contents

Acknowledgments

We were blessed with teachers from one-room school houses who came into town and graced us with their skills.

With greatest respect for Dan Newman who showed me what a true gentleman is. We shared a unique bond.

Jane Kilpatrick and I became friends in 1970. Jane gave me unique, new, and different perspectives on creativity which are still a part of me today. I'm grateful for the role she played in my life and that she played it with such gusto.

She gifted me my favorite quote by T.S. Eliot.

> We shall not cease from exploration
> And the end of all our exploring
> Will be to arrive where we started
> And know the place for the first time.

With a grateful heart for publisher Connie Taylor who guided me through the logjams and more. Sincere thanks to Rebecca McAlpine for fostering the connection.

Jodi Struble

She's my best friend who has stood by me through thick and thin. The matriarch of the family, she's a role model as a mother and grandmother. She's an intellectual, a voracious reader, and a great writer with a gift for humor. She's a long-arm quilter. She makes quilts and barn quilts, afghans, dishrags, stocking caps, you name it, anything that can be woven, sewn, or made by hand. With nothing else to do, like most quilters she solves puzzles. She prefers to listen to stories rather than music.

She's an adventurous, independent soul. She drove cross-country by herself. She camps alone in her beloved Casita. She likes wine, or scotch and water, English mysteries, anything written by P.D. James, Stephen King, J.L. Tolkein, Bernard Cornwall, Diana Gabaldon, Ann Rice. Too many to list here.

One day she found an annotated version of *War and Peace*, so she read it a second time!

Jodi cooks primal or Mediterranean. She makes wicked Jewish chicken noodle soup that's a cure for anything that ails you. She can paint a room, use a caulking gun, do wallpapering and hang pictures and shelves using a screw gun.

She has common sense and she's the best problem solver I've ever known. She's an amazing person and everyone who knows her, knows it.

She's Jodi Struble, my wife, my rock, my love, my wife of thirty-five years.

Kurt Struble
August 5, 2022

Foreword

As Kurt's high school classmate, I knew him only as an athlete, a drummer, and a boy with a devilish grin who was, (always getting into trouble) perhaps, somewhat of a goof-off.

Our paths seldom crossed. Reading works he shared on Facebook a few years ago, I was taken aback by the captivating charm of his words, seemingly so disconnected from my memories of him. When he mentioned his ADD, I asked him if he might share some of his coping mechanisms. Thus began my conversations into knowing Kurt. His efforts to control the mental wanderings and lightning-fast thoughts flowing through his mind are, and have been, truly masterful. But this thing he struggles with is also a gift. A wild and wonderful gift. Words tumble out of him and onto paper like a raging waterfall, cascading onto paper via his Gold Wing pencil. Then the work begins to tame the waters and corral each droplet into a smooth-flowing stream.

To step into these stories of a small-town mid-western boy is to experience them as if you were there. Perhaps you were. Kurt is a keeper of memories rich in vivid detail, genuine honesty, and vulnerability. There's sentimentality mixed with humor, silliness even, when he resurrects the boy within. Stories told from that boy's perspective evoke innocence and tenderness, making them both endearing and memorable. And though this was likely not the objective, you come to know and understand the man this boy became.

Forever an admirer,
Karen (Karhoff) Lewis

Michigan
The Great Lakes State
10,000 Lakes Surrounded by Glacial Seas

We Were Boomers

I'm a small-town Boomer Kid born at the midpoint of the twentieth century a few years after World War II when our parents, with the help of the infrastructure of war, reinvented America from 60% agrarian to 60% manufacturing.

Those fifteen years were the closest any civilization has ever come to perfection. We were the strongest nation in the world. There was widespread prosperity and upward mobility. We were healthy after eradicating polio, German measles, chicken pox and other diseases. Every fabric of life was being reinvented after eight years of war. We were optimistic about the future.

We had just enough technology to make life more comfortable. Television was the newest invention bringing with it an awareness of our place in the world. Usually going off the air at midnight. Through television, we defined ourselves as a nation being reborn.

We Boomer Kids lived in a bubble of security, our minds uncluttered by horror stories. Ugly, grisly stuff seen and heard today, we would have considered unthinkable.

We were free from fear. We walked or rode our bikes to school, went home for lunch and returned. We played sports by emulating older kids. Then we became models for younger kids. We shopped downtown where generations shopped before regional malls disconnected links to the past.

We Boomer Kids were free with our parent's blessing (the only requirement was to be home in time for dinner) to explore the surrounding fields and streams unhindered by busy highways around sprawling suburbs or the confines of gated communities.

We knew about life. It surrounded us. It beckoned us to join it. We eagerly accepted the invitation. Our bikes took us to where life lived. Life wrapped its arms around us.

I love my worlds. I'm happy to share my worlds with you. I hope you love them, too.

Kurt Struble
August 5, 2022

Summer

Lake Huron Shoreline
Near the Alabaster Pipeline

When I Was Born

That summer, warm and sultry,
midmonth, midyear, midway past midnight,
bright lights shining blinding,
hands grasping fingers smashing
through the air,
I did not really care,
it was not my problem.

I was theirs for the taking.

I heard the pain that wasn't mine
explode into my space,
the air, the rush of light that came before
the crack of dawn exposed the ship
that I'd been riding on
between the worlds where I once lived
when I was born!

With great surprise, I threw away my aqua lungs.
I sucked in air while water flooded,
breathing synapses firing newborn pistons.
Two-hundred eighty-three horses blowing
streams of light in all directions.
So, this is what it's like to live in the land of milk and honey!

Come time to leave for home,
I looked into the sky I'd never seen,
acorns falling through the air,
cool harmonies on the breeze singing memories

3

from where it all began,
wrapped around light
that fuels the seeds of future's flight,
while tightly-woven earthly patterns
leading everywhere in sight
bring great brilliance and such delight!

Each night, I see the world inside my dreams
wrapped inside the morning dew.
Each morning, my life begins anew,
never sure of all that I have seen until
I return and do it all again,
and again, and again,
until I think,
therefore,
I am.

To Summer Boy

During summers, I had the freedom
to range freely about town
searching for other boys,
looking for one more kid
to round off an even number
for a game of tackle football
or three-against-three baseball.

On special days,
I meet up with my best friend.

We ride our bikes
three to five miles out of town
over blacktop and gravel roads,
passing open fields
to creek water flowing
under a wooden bridge.

We wade through gravel beds
flecked with pieces of mica
flashing golden in the sun,
searching for crawdads or anything living
we could hold in the palms of our hands,
our eyes boring deeper and deeper
into life's details until
we could almost see
the light
within.

Before There Were S'mores

Once upon an early summer evening time, the sun's orange light barely visible setting in the western sky behind the trees, I decide to take a walk along the shoreline of the Great Lake before bedtime.

Gray, my faithful Weimaraner dog, comes to life as soon as I head toward the back door, prancing and pacing, up and down on her front paws. Her short tail seems to wag her entire body. Softly keening with a hopeful smile on her face, she pleads with me to take her along.

"Sorry. Not this time, Gray," I say exiting the screened door at the back of the cottage.

Rounding the back corner, halfway along the side, the backdoor slams, ricochets, coming to rest a second time. From inside the house, I hear Mom reminding me for the umpteenth time, "Don't let the screen door slam shut!"

When I step onto the sandy path leading up to the lake, the first thing I see is a big fire on the top of the sand dune leading down to the beach and the water's edge.

A family of five: two brothers, a younger sister, and their parents who spend summers in the cottage next door are gathered around the fire.

They're laughing, and playing, and shouting funny jokes, making fun of each other, having a great time. The parents look on with bright smiles, laughing hardest of all at the antics of their kids.

They don't know me but they've seen me. I don't know them except for the little sister who's annoying, since whenever she sees me, she wants to tag along, which is fine, but she never stops talking. When the little sister sees me, she talks to her parents, then walks toward me.

"Hi!" she says. "We're roasting marshmallows, would you like to join us?"

The rest of the group chimes in saying, "Yes, please come and join us."

I like marshmallows and everything like that, but I've never tasted a roasted marshmallow. I have no idea what a roasted marshmallow is or even looks like. I'm too embarrassed to ask but of course, to be mannerly, I accept their invitation.

So, I go to the fire and stand between the older brother and the little sister where I watch everyone talk, and laugh, and dance around acting silly. At first, I feel like everyone's watching me so I'm afraid to say anything.

But it's easy to laugh at some of the things they do and say, especially when they all gang up and tease the little sister because she never stops talking. Even I laugh at her. But I don't think she cares. The smile she carries around lights up even more when she's the center of attention.

Pretty soon, I'm laughing along and feeling relaxed like they've made me part of their family. I might have even made a couple of funny comments myself!

After fifteen or twenty minutes, I decide to take a rest and watch everyone for a little while. So I take a seat on a big log apart from the group next to the fire. While seated, my attention is riveted to each individual face, fascinated by their ever-changing appearances; the reflected light of the fire giving ghoulish expressions or a copper-colored glow that momentarily makes them look beautiful.

The night is cool because it's early summer, but the fire feels warm, so the goose bumps on my arms have disappeared and I feel warm and comfortable.

The onshore breeze touching my face and shoulders feels refreshing on my first sunburn of the summer. I hear the lake whispering behind me from tiny whitecaps breaking at the shoreline. I look up and see an immense star-filled, navy-blue sky bigger than any sky I've ever seen; the Big Dipper and the North Star clearly visible.

Between the fire and the laughter and the night sky and the swish of the waves, it seems the cool breeze has wrapped itself around and joined everything together. I'm experiencing feelings never felt before.

While I, a ten-year-old boy on summer vacation, am enjoying these special new feelings, the little sister, while talking non-stop, walks around the circle giving everyone, including me, a bag of marshmallows.

The younger brother follows behind, passing out metal prongs with two pointed tines on one end with a wood-handle grip. The kind you'd use to cook a hot dog over an open fire.

Curious, having never even **seen** a roasted marshmallow, I watch closely as everyone takes one or two, sticks them through the metal points, then holds the marshmallows over the flames. I watch them turn beautiful shades of tan, then darker tan with spots like a leopard. If held over the fire too long, the leopard spots bleed into each other, turn black, and burn with a pale-yellow flame. Everyone seems to enjoy the burned marshmallows as much as the others!

This I cannot understand!

I watch the younger brother remove his from the fire, blow out the flame, wait a second or so, then blow a second time to cool it.

Opening wide with puckered lips, he pulls a marshmallow off the metal prong while closing his eyes. Within seconds, a satisfied smile appears on his face while reaching into the bag for two more.

I don't know what to do next. My inexperience must have been obvious. After the older brother swallows, he asks if I've ever roasted a marshmallow and would I like to try one? I'm not sure how I feel about them. The colors are beautiful but I don't think they look that great after catching fire and turning black.

But to be mannerly, I say, "Okay."

Before I even finish sliding the marshmallows onto the pointed tines, I hear the little sister telling me how to hold it close to the flame, but not too close. By the time I put my prong into the flames, she has told me the same thing three different ways which is pretty annoying because I had already seen everybody roast theirs over the fire, so I should know how by now. The rest of the group laughs while watching our exchange.

While everyone watches, I slowly roast my first marshmallow back and forth over the embers and flames of the fire. When it turns golden brown, I see bubbles on the surface that turn blackish while the white becomes a dark tan burning with a soft-yellow flame.

The little girl pleads, "Take it out of the fire or it'll be too burned to eat!" So, I move the marshmallow away from the fire.

Clapping her hands with excitement, the little sister says, "Now blow on it, blow on it and eat it!" She's being fairly annoying since what else can I do but blow it out and eat it like I'd seen everyone do? Once again everyone's laughing because they know how annoying she can be, but they also know how funny she is.

But it doesn't matter because I'm focused on what will happen next.

I blow on the marshmallow a couple of times like I've seen the others do. I lightly touch it to my upper lip to make sure it's not too hot. I don't want to burn the inside of my mouth. I close my mouth over the black surface, pucker my lips, and slide the tine out of the marshmallow, leaving only the marshmallow inside my mouth.

Then I have a **big** surprise! It doesn't taste anything like I thought it would taste!

The flakey surface of the marshmallow tastes like very thin caramel-flavored paper. To my surprise, the inside is melted and warm and creamy. I taste an incredible combination of flavors; warm and sweet with a smokey aftertaste as the thin burnt paper dissolves.

The marshmallow invades my body with sugar flowing 'round my tongue, and gums, and teeth, and the roof of my mouth. The sides of my tongue luxuriate swimming through the mixture. An alarm clock rings loudly inside my brain. Every fiber in my body wakes up screaming, "Sweet, so sweet! Caramel! Flavored sugar paper, ummm. This is so good!"

Closing my eyes, I tilt my head back luxuriating in this new sweet flavor, warm and creamy. "Ummm," I hear my own low tones as the delicious concoction trickles down my throat seeping into my body.

I'd never tasted anything so deliciously sweet in my entire life! Lowering my head with opened eyes, I realize everyone is laughing and pointing at me.

The little sister claps her hands while jumping up and down at the same time! "Look at his face! Look at his face!" she squeals.

Everyone seems happy to have introduced me to this new treat, delighted by the pleasure on my face and the pleasurable sounds I make. Happy they could share their warm laughter and silliness with me. I've carried a piece of those warm feelings around with me for the rest of my life.

I've had hundreds, perhaps thousands, of roasted marshmallows since that night, and some pretty good s'mores, too. I still love to tell about the first time I ate a roasted marshmallow with a laughing family acting silly, having fun while standing next to a big fire on top of a sand dune, next to the Great Lake, on an early summer evening with the stars above while a cool breeze joined everything together.

And I always tell everyone I'm with, "And that was the **best** roasted marshmallow I ever ate!"

Primordia

The Great Lake
Along the Eastern Shoreline

We pitched our tents between the dunes,
behind a stretch of gnarly evergreens,
tempering onshore breezes
blowing off the glacial sea,
moving and alive.
Her ever-present hypnosis
the sound of miniature curls
lapping the shore.

An Endless Exchange

Walking north along her shoreline,
Great Lake's water breathing
slow and steady to my right
in a world of white caps dimly lighted,
no demarcation seen
between water and darkening gray
except its bristly surface waiting to explode
with silent rising to pale blue skies
or streaks of orange and gray
reaching across the eastern sky
from morning sun.

11

Her roiling black underbelly in stormy reflection
hiding until the time is right,
stretching wings before flight,
an endless exchange.

A Living Entity

Left of where I walk,
pale green grasses grow sparsely
among sandy hills.
Behind dunes further west
on risen ground,
tall pines grow in darker soil
waiting for new life to begin.

She's the Great Lake along
the eastern shoreline,
a living entity!

When she breathes, swells rise up,
heaving with motion,
exploding into white caps,
each wave torn asunder.

Or she laps her waves silently
with farewell kisses to rocks and boulders,
surrendering their immensity
from shale and granite, quartz crystal
and sediment, to grains of sand overlaid
with prismatic color, scourged from earth,
pushed ashore, each grain a tiny atom
from the union of water, ice, and stone
broken down over millennia.

She's my friend since early childhood innocence
when I wandered into her world.
A steady hand I've played within
on days she held me in her grasp
allowing me to peek through windows
into her glacial past.

Primordia

She's always beautiful
but even more so
when she lets her fury reign,
returning to Primordia
with perfect remembrance
of her violent past.
A splendid reminder of her purest self.
A return from whence she came.

Perfect Prizes

Among visions seen inside that night
a dozen or more alive within my sight
to a place where time was small,
when bright light filled all
with purest boyhood memories.
Where sun and single pleasure meet
from place of innocent splendor,
I seek to look upon the Great Lake's face with wonder;
light stained against the sky of thought,
suspended in time,
hovering over each place
for me to move and turnabout
in all the places
I still can see.

Perfect prizes captured
for me to live in
momentarily.

Raising the Crane

How a Boy Learns about Life and Death

My awareness of life and death began one afternoon on a typical summer day in northern Michigan, temperature around eighty-two, the air blown clean and crystal clear by northern breezes, a pale blue sky under a mid-season sun struggling to stay white, halfway through the summer, on Tawas Point also known as "The Point," a tapering finger of dunes, scrub oak, and gnarly pines extending into Lake Huron,[1] wrapped around Tawas Bay where I spent three summers at the family cottage.

Ours was the second one back from the lake across an open field from the U.S. Coast Guard Station. A sandy two-lane path across the front of the cottage rose, then gently dropped, to a wide, tan-colored beach at the Great Lake's shoreline where all the stories begin.

Earlier at Jerry's Marina

Gliding over the dock at Jerry's Marina that day, the tires of my bicycle playing a steady 4/4 beat in concert with two-by-fours rolling under my tires, I look into their rented, round-bottom boats tied to the dock, on my way to no place in particular at that particular time.

I see ropes and anchors, open tackle boxes, daredevils and jitterbugs strewn alongside fish scalers, dead "minnies" stuck to aluminum gunwales, empty Schlitz and Strohs beer cans, stringers with twenty or thirty yellow perch, covered with flies, drying in the sun; each fish the prize for a day spent guzzling beer while dropping baited hooks into the chop of the bay. By the time I realize I'm riding too slow to stay upright, it's too late. I lose momentum, pitch over sideways, falling into murky marina water, bicycle and all!

1 Third largest Great Lake along the east coast of the lower peninsula of Michigan.

Bobbing to the surface, a thick, meaty hand greets me. A deep voice says, "Can I help you up, Son?" First, my bike rises from the oily depths. Then comes me, dripping with oil and water.

Intent on escaping my embarrassment, I ride away so quickly that I barely hear myself say thank you to the man who rescued me. And so, the story begins.

Discovering the Crane

I stood on the shoreline of the bay that day, ten years old, gazing over at Jerry's Marina, a hundred yards south, my clothes still damp, the embarrassment of having to be rescued still fresh in my mind.

"Oh well." I shrug my shoulders, turn, and begin walking north on the lime-rock road alongside a deep swale to my left toward the blacktop that will take Gray (my Weimaraner dog and constant companion) and me back to the cottage where we will probably spend the rest of the day swimming in the Great Lake.

Gray sloshes in a foot or so of water at the bottom of the swale trying to pick up the scent of some animal within the thick growth of cattails when I hear her barking non-stop.

Gray's Discovery

I trot along until I see Gray barking at a giant water crane, its head taller than the cattails, standing in shallow water at the bottom of the swale, where it was probably hunting for frogs, when Gray made her discovery. Gray continues barking while circling the crane, occasionally pausing to sniff or nip at its leg.

The crane looks unafraid, strangely motionless, seemingly unaware of the dog's barking or my presence. So, I decide to take a closer look.

Soaking in the Details

I ditch my bike in the weeds, slide down the embankment, and creep through the cattails, careful not to make sudden movements or splash water.

The crane slowly curls its long neck into a flattened s-shape, the back half resting along its spine, its head and beak in profile.

Suddenly it occurs to me that if I take one more step, the big bird might fly away. I never thought I'd be so close to such a magnificent creature. I want to see all the details before it's too late. I freeze all movement perhaps fifteen feet away. Hopefully the big bird will stay grounded so I can take a closer look.

Admiring

I admire the curve of its skull, the tiny nostrils on each side of its beak, perhaps ten-twelve inches long, red mini feathers dancing in the wind on the crown of its head. I see tiny scales covering its stick-like legs, each smaller than a dime, overlapping themselves like tiny shingles, smooth, aerodynamic in design.

I look at the variations of gray coloring along the short hairs of its neck that gradually lengthen into six-to-twelve-inch feathers covering its wings, so large that they stretch the length of its entire body from its breastbone to the shorter soft feathers on the backside, lying next to each other, slightly overlapped like a tightly louvered fan pointing downward while standing.

Feathers, Clouds, Wind

I picture its wings in flight, the shorter, round feathers at the back edge vibrating or fluttering through the air like the sensitive fingers of a pianist each in tune with the incremental movements needed to stabilize and direct the strength it takes to create forward thrust. Their giant wings beat downward, pushing the great birds upward in graceful flight gliding through the air on chimneys of warm air, two different parts of its body telling it what to do; the breastbone and the long tail feathers telling it to rise up and up, effortlessly higher and higher. Flying free over clouds of air, *they see* what we *can only imagine*.

I creep forward cautiously until we stand a few feet apart. I sense a strangeness about its lack of movement as if it's in a trance.

Crane's Eye Seeking Awareness

I look closely into its eye, the iris a thin-orange/blood-red ribbon surrounding the pupil so large it nearly fills the entire eye socket, a dark, black pool without a flicker of life.

While looking into its eye, I think how great it would be to see some sense of awareness. Something that would tell me the crane isn't dead or dying. When suddenly, it breaks out of its trance. Its pupil flickers, a spark of sunlight reflects off of the surface of the black pool. The iris contracts; the dark pool grows smaller until it finds a focal point.

It's Alive, It Has Awareness!

I watch its eye tracking from place-to-place over my face feeling bewildered perhaps by my curious movements, the soft shapes and colors of my face, filling its awareness with sights different from its everyday world gliding high, looking down at ponds and streams, wading through water, searching, always searching to satisfy the hunger that gives life meaning. The desire to live.

Suddenly, I know it's alive! It has awareness. I feel a link between our searching, ever-curious minds.

Cradling the Crane

Emboldened by the crane's lack of aggression, I move closer, wrap both arms beneath its belly, lift it out of the water, then struggle to carry it up the slippery slope onto the lime-rock road. A short distance later, I turn right onto the blacktop and walk east toward the cottage cradling the bird in my arms, trying to see over the hump of its back, feeling its wing feathers against my chin, the short feathers along its neck tickling the side of my face.

I try to stay focused on the road ahead, straining to keep the bird's talons from scraping the blacktop, oblivious of the passing cars, their honking horns, stupid comments and questions.

Gray trots along beside me keeping a wary eye out for my safety. The bird, its neck fully extended, gazes at the passing trees and empty spaces along the side of the road.

Walking along, I picture myself nursing the bird back to health; feeding it, loving it, giving it life once again, then watching it fly away, free to ride the wind currents, once again aware of its world with a renewed desire to live.

Baby Squirrels

I had watched Mom raise six baby squirrels from the time they were hairless, no bigger than the end of her pinky finger, feeding them every four hours, twenty-four hours a day for weeks until they grew and became such a nuisance. All six of them climbed over her body like she was a small tree, tangling her hair, knocking her glasses off. She finally gave them freedom.

Surely, she would help me rescue the bird.

I had high hopes for my friend, the great crane, who had allowed me to gaze into its eye and be part of its life.

Lowering the Crane

Back at the cottage, I lower the crane onto the sand in the open field. The instant its feet touch the ground, its head drops back into the s-position. Before running to the back to tell Mom, I take another look into the crane's eye. Instead of the flicker of awareness I had seen earlier, I see the same blank stare as when I first looked into its eye.

I run to the back of the cottage where, with great excitement, I tell Mom about the big bird. I tell her how beautiful it is. "Maybe it's sick," I tell her, "but, we can feed it frogs, nurse it back to health like you did with the baby squirrels."

Anxious to get back to the crane, I don't take time to answer any of her questions. Instead, I turn and run toward the front of the cottage. "Wait 'til you see how beautiful it is!" I shout over my shoulder.

An Unexpected Surprise: Eyes the Size of Silver Dollars

Seeing the crane, touching it, carrying it, made the crane a familiar part of my world. I should have known first sight of the big bird would be an unexpected surprise for Mom. The sight of me standing next to the six-foot bird stops her dead in her tracks at the corner of the cottage where she stands motionless.

Her eyes are the size of silver dollars, her jaw drops open, her body in half stride, in suspended animation her eyes move back and forth between the crane and me, a sense of wonder and bewilderment on her face. She's too shocked to take one step further or even say a word.

She Strokes Its Neck

To reassure her, I stand next to the crane, lightly touching its back.

The big bird opens its eyes, unfurls its long neck while slowly turning its head left-to-right before staring straight ahead, motionless.

Mom can't resist the urge to touch the big bird. She cautiously approaches. She caresses its long neck with the back of her hand speaking to it in low tones, while asking me stupid questions like, "Did the bird act like it was sick?" or, "Did it seem like the bird wanted to stab you in the eye?"

Jake Willis

I sense her feelings are warming to the thought of nursing the bird back to health. "Well golly, Mom. I don't know. I've never made friends with a sick bird before."

She smiles. It seems a chink in her armor has opened when Jake Willis, the old guy living on the opposite side of the curve, three houses further west, appears. The three of us gaze at the big bird, each wondering what to do next.

Jake doesn't say much. He squints at the crane, his thumb and index finger moving along his chin line, deep in thought.

Mom breaks the silence, repeating her earlier concern that the bird could be sick. Only this time, she looks to Jake for confirmation.

Jake asks me if the bird tried to stab me in the eye. I feel like saying "Do I look like a fish or a frog?" Instead, I stare at him, a crooked smile on my face, a slight movement of my head from left to right.

They both insist the bird could have blinded me. They tell me the bird is too sick to live. I hate them for saying this. Who are they to decide whether another creature should live or die?

They look at each other, then back at me. Without a word, I know the verdict.

Waiting for Death

I follow Jake to his house where I sit hunched over on an old wooden bench made from two tree stumps and a thick board facing eastward toward the lake. I wait for Jake to emerge from the side door of his house, not knowing what to expect.

Halfway between where I sit and the top of a dune at the far end of the lane, the crane stands motionless on one spindly leg, the left side of its body in profile, its long neck and beak sharply defined.

The lake appears as a grayish-blue ribbon between the top of the dune and the pale blue afternoon sky reflecting off the horizon line.

The crane appears lifeless now, almost like a statue. Maybe the flicker of awareness I thought I had seen when I stared into its unblinking eye was my imagination? Had we really made a connection back in the swale where Gray made her discovery?

I hear the door click shut as Jake approaches.

Jake's Gun

The double barrels of Jake's shotgun point skyward to my left. Jake lowers the gun barrels so they're pointing at the ground. With his thumb against the locking lever, he jerks the gun up sharply. The shotgun cracks open looking like it's broken. The barrels look like a couple of black holes.

Jake cradles the open shotgun against the left side of his body. With one continuous motion, I hear the "thunk, thunk" of the shells dropping into the chamber. Jake pulls up while pushing down at the same time locking the double barrels into place.

The barrels move upward disappearing from my field of vision. Jake walks six or seven paces closer to the bird. I see Jake's back and the barrel above his left shoulder. I continue staring straight ahead at the bird, its red head feathers fluttering in the breeze like they did when I first saw the big crane back in the swale after Gray's discovery brought us together.

Red Feathers

I can't take my eyes off of those dancing red feathers. It feels like I'm in two places at the same time. I'm sitting on a stoop along the side of Jake's house waiting for what will happen next and I'm at the bottom of the swale where I first saw those dancing red feathers.

In some strange way, maybe those feathers are an acknowledgment that there **had** been a connection between us. Things can be funny like that sometimes, don't you think?

Silence fills the air. Jake's body becomes frozen in place. The gun rests between his cheek and shoulder, his right elbow pointed slightly downward. His right index finger unseen, curls around the trigger of the big gun.

I can't even hear myself breathing because I'm holding my breath. I feel frozen in place and time, unable to move a muscle when, without warning, an explosion lifts me off my seat! I tip over backward but manage to regain my balance.

The shotgun's explosion rocks my world. I've just witnessed the most amazing sight I've ever seen.

To Look More Closely

I need to look more closely at the bird to satisfy my curiosity. When Jake's gun exploded, the crane must have dropped to the earth so instantaneously, it appeared to simply disappear.

I walk toward the mound of gray feathers where the bird once stood, anxious to see what it looks like. Strangely, I have a hard time distinguishing the bird from the surroundings where it lies.

The head and beak of what used to be the beautiful bird lie in profile, flat against the sand. The black iris I looked into less than an hour ago when sensing its awareness, covered now with an opaque film over its lifeless eye, the head and beak and neck inanimate objects attached to a mound of gray feathers. A few of the shorter feathers lifting in the breeze look like they're holding onto some memory. The object of their lives lying flat against the sand, the process of absorption having already begun; the force of gravity returning what's left of my friend, the crane, into the earth.

The Shot That Rocked My World

I still think about what happened back then. When Jake fired the shot that rocked my world, I had no idea the bird would simply disappear.

Looking back, I don't know what I expected to see after Jake shot the bird. I **did not** think the big bird would disappear when it died. Even lying on the ground after being killed, it was not the same bird. The real bird had disappeared. This is what I came away with after my first encounter with death in the so-called *real world*.

Death? It's when life disappears! With that in mind, I wrote this poem about death.

Where Life Goes

Where life goes is
everyone's guess!
I suppose *I* don't know
where life goes, but
its got to go somewhere,
don't you think?

I'd hate to think it just
comes and goes
after being inside us,
with nowhere else to go.

Each life, a drop of matter containing
our memories and revelations,
floating through the oceanic depths of space
within an infinite sea of time.

Don't you think it should be more than **that!?**

To Kill an Oath

While gazing down at my friend the crane, I make a solemn oath to myself: When it comes to stealing life away—human or beast—we should participate to the *least* extent possible. It's best to let nature take care of herself without interference whenever we can, out of respect for life!

It's not until afterward that I realize maybe I should have convinced Jake and Mom to let me take the crane back where I found it so it could die the way nature intended. This is when I realized their decision to kill the bird was adult thinking at its worst. But then, who am I to judge? Maybe I shouldn't have carried my friend, the crane, home in the first place?

But at *least* I'll *know better* when *I* grow up and face similar circumstances.

What Is Life?

Later, Mom cooks hamburgers on the little gas stove in the kitchen at the back of the cottage. Jake is probably nodding off in his easy chair, an open *Detroit Free Press* stretched across his chest. I'm still outside in the gloaming looking down, observing the bird, remembering all that happened, pondering the introduction of thoughts and feelings that come with first-time experiences; the nature of life and death, the purpose of life. A new awareness of the universal mystery: What is life?

It's almost dark now. Mom is calling me for dinner. I turn and walk to the front corner of the cottage. In a minute, I'll go through the screen door at the back of the cottage, careful not to let it slam shut. I'll enter the eat-in kitchen where Mom has cooked my favorite meal; two hamburgers, fried potatoes with corn on the cob, and a tall glass of milk.

As I round the corner, I stop. I turn and take one last look at the crane. I add one more provision to my solemn oath about life. I even hear myself say it out loud!

"And I'll never grow up and start thinking like an adult."

And do you know what?

I never did.

The Amphibian

Occasionally the Amphibian rises from the lake,
climbs the dune, then
clamors along the sandy lane
in front of the cottage.

If lucky, we get to see it lumbering by,
dripping water, its propellers still spinning,
balanced on six huge tires, three on each side,
clustered in the middle,
taller than me!

Its two powerful diesel engines
vibrate the air with sound
and power.

Thick black smoke blows rearward
from two chromed exhaust pipes
six to eight feet above the cab.
The top half of the driver's face,
peering through three narrow windows
and the scared faces of ten men
can be seen through five portholes
on both sides as the vehicle
slowly passes by.

24

Within minutes,
the Amphibian Rescue Vehicle
disappears around the curve
two beach houses west of ours.
The only remnant of its presence,
the decrescendo of its twin diesels
moving toward the lime-rock road
I ride on to go fishing.

And a black haze of smoke slowly moving west,
pushed along by an onshore breeze,
blown off the lake
before only silence
fills the
air.

Exploding the Cracker

The Roland brothers, Karl and Keith, live in a log house with a picture window, five or ten minutes from the cottage, west along the blacktop road, leading to Jerry's Marina. Most mornings, I buy candy (Black Jacks, Dots, Maple-Flavored Bun candy bars) or minnows when I go fishing.

Opposite the Roland house, across a narrow blacktop, a one-lane, lime-rock road stretches a half mile to the U.S. Coast Guard Boathouse. The Boathouse sits on huge wooden pilings a hundred yards into Tawas Bay connected to the lime-rock road by a wide wooden dock. I fish along the south wall of the boathouse happy to catch a few perch, smallmouth bass, or a lake trout.

This adventure begins next to the Roland brothers' house where there's a small pond.

Exploring Live-Bait Minnows

I don't see the Roland brothers very often, but when I do, we always end up doing the same thing: exploring around the edges of the minnow pond next to their house where Jerry's Marina stores live-bait minnows.

They love to explore nature as much as I do. We spend hours creeping through pond grass around the pond seeking insect eggs, or bird's nests, snakes, you name it.

We wade through cattails, pushing them aside searching for anything alive and interesting we can catch and look at more closely. We look under dead logs for red and yellow salamanders or garter snakes slithering through the grass. We step on their tails and pinch them behind their heads to look into their reptile eyes. We study their slithering, forked tongues, careful not to touch their bodies or they'll secrete the foulest smelling pee you can imagine.

There's plenty of excitement even when discovering something we've seen dozens of times before: swarms of tadpoles gliding through the water turning this way and that, the same as flocks of birds. Near the shoreline where the water is warm, we find clusters of frog eggs looking like tiny bubbles of air with a black dot inside. They're clustered together nestled within wisps of algae looking like green clouds in different stages of development, somehow clinging to the sandy bottom.

As the black dot slowly grows, it occupies more space inside the clear BB-sized eggs. Just before hatching, the black dots appear as tiny pollywogs occupying all the space inside the BB-sized eggs. When they outgrow their enclosures, they turn into full-fledged pollywogs able to breathe underwater like a fish!

Later the polliwogs, or tadpoles, change into frogs. Which is amazing! We often wonder, how do they do it? We've never seen a single tadpole turn into a frog, although we have seen larger tadpoles with much shorter tails swimming around with legs sticking out of their sides.

After much discussion, we decided that tadpoles probably turn into frogs during the night when they make such a racket all night long talking or singing, or maybe even celebrating, because they've finally become frogs!

Suddenly these big black pollywogs with legs and skinny tails no longer live exclusively under water breathing like fish. They become the frogs we call "green leapers" breathing air as we do, unable to breathe underwater.

We call these frogs "green leapers" for good reason. They can leap three-or-four feet to avoid capture if they detect the slightest sound or movement which makes them very hard to catch.

Once discovered hiding in the grass, their backs arched, heads pointing down, hiding, you have to creep up on them very slowly holding your breath. They seem to have eyes in the back of their heads or maybe they can swivel their bulging eyes backward to see what's in back of them! Their muscular legs always cocked and ready to go, enables them to suddenly spring two or three feet from your cupped hand at the slightest hint of a shadow or the softest sound.

When one is captured, we gather shoulder-to-shoulder touching its glossy skin, fascinated by its green markings, the texture of its undersides, the flat, round, drum-like membranes on both sides of its head looking like eardrums. If its belly is fat and wide, we wonder what kind of insect they're digesting inside.

Karl's Discovery

One day while Keith and I were walking behind Karl after a couple hours of exploring, we watch Karl pull something out from the weeds alongside the road. About the size of a cigarette, Karl twists the object around in his fingers examining it more closely.

Naturally, our curiosity is aroused.

When Keith and I catch up, the three of us, our necks extended, peer down at what Karl holds between his fingers.

"It's a firecracker!" says Karl. "But it doesn't have a fuse."

After quietly looking at the strange Chinese lettering on the side, we talk excitedly about how much fun it would be to watch it explode. Disappointed, when the reality of the missing fuse becomes apparent, our dreams of exploding the firecracker momentarily go up in smoke.

Undeterred, Karl holds the firecracker in front of us as we continue walking in deep thought, back to their house. We sit cross-legged facing each other on the sandy driveway discussing different ways to explode the firecracker.

Putting Our Heads Together

I suggest lighting a match inserted into the end of the firecracker. Keith thinks it's a great idea but Karl reminds him, "There aren't any matches in the house 'cause Pops uses a lighter to light his cigarettes."

Oh ... shoot. I forgot.

Things get quiet. Then Keith remembers the time they burned holes in leaves using the magnifying glass Pops uses to read the newspaper. "We could put the firecracker inside some twigs and leaves and use the magnifying glass to start the fire."

Keith looks at us with pleading eyes. Karl and I silently nod our heads while staring at the firecracker.

"It might just work," Karl says under his breath.

We nod our heads in silent agreement while staring down at the cracker.

"See! If I'm a lily-livered rooster pecker, then so are you! Because I'm just as smart as you or even smarter." Keith looks at Karl with a smile of equanimity. Without saying another word, Karl heads for the front door to retrieve the magnifying glass while Keith and I scrounge around looking for small sticks or pieces of newspaper.

When Karl returns with the magnifying glass, he forms a mound of sand. The firecracker stands straight up on top of the mound looking like it's a miniature stick of dynamite plugging up the hole at the top of a volcano.

How to Build a Fire

By the time I return with a piece of newspaper and some dead grass, Karl and Keith have made a mess out of building a fire putting sticks haphazardly all around the firecracker.

"You'll never get a fire started like that," I say. "You'll smother it. I'll show you how Dad showed me."

While disassembling their work, I explain, "You have to build a little tepee with newspaper and dried grass, then sticks over the top. The tepee sucks air from the bottom feeding the flames so the sticks will catch fire."

Like a Twisting Snake

With their work completely disassembled, I crumple up and lay newspaper around the bottom of the mound, grass over the newspaper then small twigs standing on end, leaning against each other, lying flat, resting against the mound.

Keith and I watch while Karl, stretched out on his stomach, positions himself in a perfect place to capture heat from the sun's rays. Karl focuses the light until a tiny white dot appears on a piece of newspaper. Seconds later, a black dot appears. Keith and I, already on our hands and knees, lean forward closer to the curling smoke, eager to see if our solution works. White smoke appears from the black dot, curling its way upward like a twisting snake.

Orange Light Wrapped Around a Circle

The black dot quickly forms into a larger hole, black around the edges. Karl blows gently. An orange light flickers and quickly joins itself around the circumference of the hole. The flickering orange hole continues to grow in size and brightness. Karl continues blowing. The hole continues growing. When it's the size of a pencil eraser, tiny flames rise up. There's more smoke and flame as the newspaper starts burning.

As if hypnotized, we can't take our eyes off the flames growing larger as the fire consumes more fuel.

Suddenly, Keith says, "I'm gettin' out of here."

I look up at Keith. Rising to his feet, he continues staring at the burning flame as if hypnotized **Bamm! Snap! Wham! Crack! Boom!**

The sand blasting against my face feels like a million pin pricks. It feels like I'm being pushed backward by a powerful force. I find myself lying on my back, fists pressed against my eyes, my world turned black, afraid to open them for fear I'll be blind.

My ears are ringing with a high-pitched "Weeeeeeeeeeeeee" that doesn't let up. Now I'm thinking, "Could I be blind **and** deaf?"

The Sound of Running Water

Keith's voice and the sound of running water help me navigate toward the outdoor spigot where there's a hose on the side of their house. Making my way toward the sound of the water, my hand extended, I take a chance and briefly open one eye. The world looks blurred. It feels like I've scratched my eyes but I'm confident once I get the sand out, I'll be okay.

Cool Water Cascading

While waiting for Karl to finish, I take my t-shirt off and shake it. Sand flies everywhere prickling my face and chest.

When it's my turn, I bend at the waist, letting the cool water cascade over the crown of my head, down across my neck. I move the hose forward. The water wraps itself around the sides of my face, dripping off my cheeks. I tilt my head back letting the water drop onto my forehead where it flows around my closed eyes, forming rivers around my nostrils, water falls over my lips, a leaky faucet dripping from the middle of my chin.

No Easy Task

I move the hose left-to-right over my chest using my hand to push away any remaining sand, not caring if my jeans get wet. They'll dry quickly enough in the summer sun.

Finally, I have to face the music. I force myself to open my eyes and bubble water upward directly onto my eyeballs. Not an easy task for me! As much as I love to swim, I can't even open my eyes when I'm submerged in the crystal-clear water of the Great Lake!

I let the water bubble upward into my eyes, slowly forcing them to open one at a time, as wide as I can. In between washings, I look around and blink about a hundred times. It doesn't take long for me to realize I won't be blind for the rest of my life.

While Keith uses the hose to wash himself, I pull my t-shirt on and wait. When we're all finished, without saying a word, we move toward the scene of the explosion, anxious to see the crater we know the firecracker must have made.

Gazing at the Crater

Silently, the three of us gaze down at the crater. We're all thinking the same thing but no one wants to say anything. Karl breaks the ice. "That's a lot of sand we ate for lunch today, ain't it?"

We start laughing like a water faucet was just turned on. With sheepish sidelong glances, we silently acknowledge how crazy, funny, ridiculous, dumb, and stupid we were to have put our faces within blasting distance of an exploding firecracker!

"If anyone asks, I'll tell them we were curious. We wanted to do a scientific experiment to see what an actual explosion looks like, up close."

Karl laughs, "Ha-ha-ha. If that's science, you should join the army."

As if on cue, we burst out laughing while dancing around like a bunch of wild yahoos. We punch each other on the shoulder. We whoop and holler and cackle with laughter, each of us reliving the experience from our own standpoint.

We point at each other's faces telling the other how dumb we are, but no one cares. With plenty of blame to go around, we all feel equally dumb.

Figaro T. Cat

Being the older brother by two years has its advantages. For one thing, it's a lot easier for me to get my younger brother's goat than it is for him to get mine. Except on one occasion when the tables were turned in spectacular fashion.

I still have the scar to prove it!

It happened one mid-summer day up north in northern Michigan out on "The Point" across from the Coast Guard Station where the cottage is located. I was sitting in the tiny bathroom (big enough for a commode and a stand-up shower, the door within a couple feet of my knees) minding my own business, more or less waiting for movement to happen, so I could go back outside when suddenly, without warning, the door flies open.

I look up. There's my brother Kris standing in front of me, a maniacal look in his eyes (part anger, part wicked revenge, part humor) holding our black and white long-haired cat, Figaro, under her arms, her body stretched downward, her tummy exposed, yowling and growling and hissing while struggling to escape, kicking her back feet upward, her sharp claws exposed.

A Weapon to Rip My Skin to Shreds

I barely have time to think when I realize he'll be using the cat's anger coupled with its sharp claws as a weapon to rip my skin to shreds!

I can see it in his eyes!

Kris's first-degree assault with feline-intent-to-wound is well planned. Like a SAM missile, his eyes lock onto the exposed area above my knees, on top of my thighs.

I hear myself yelling like a banshee, **"No oo oo oo oo oo o!"**

He laughs, rubbing the cat's belly even harder. The cat yowls and spits with even greater intensity. I rise to defend against the vicious flesh-shredding cat but ... too late.

Kris lets fly with the cat, dropping her directly onto my exposed thighs. I watch helplessly as the cat descends like a flying squirrel with four sets of claws and a mouthful of needle-like teeth. I hear the door click shut trapping the furious cat and my fear-stricken self, inside the tiny room.

One of the cat's talons rips across my thigh just above my right knee. It feels like a high-speed jet of boiling water shot through a hypodermic needle. The stinging sensation keeps getting worse.

Meanwhile, *I'm still trapped inside a tiny room with a meshugana-crazy cat on the brink of insanity* who associates ME with the rage and frustration felt from having her tummy violently rubbed moments ago.

Desperate to escape, the cat uses her claws like crampons, gripping the walls or jumping like a mountain goat from towel rack to door knob, the sink, or anywhere she can gain a foothold. The cat streaks 'round and 'round the tiny bathroom, faster and faster, growing more desperate to escape with each passing moment.

She reminds me of those daredevil motorcyclists who ride around the inside walls of those wooden structures that look like stubby silos with no roof.

Trapped in the Eyeball of a Cat!

I can't help but think, *I'm trapped like a rat inside the eyeball of cat tornado!*

During one frantic go 'round, she slips and falls after pushing off on a hand towel lying on top of the toilet tank. On the way down, her little feet scurry like she's trying to run up a sheet of ice.

She nails a four-point landing in a crouch, springs forward, comes to rest, her left haunch against the door, her tail pointing straight up, glaring at me with a glint of hatred in her eyes, her teeth white and pointed, her mouth wide as hinges will permit, her spikey tongue quite visible. She's in a constant state of hissing, the occasional spit thrown in for emphasis.

Blood Slowly Fills the Valley of Flesh

I slowly lean forward, turn the knob, give the door a light push while staring down at a cleanly sliced, v-shaped, six-inch-flesh wound just north of my knee toward the inside of my thigh.

The cat becomes a distant memory as I watch blood slowly fill the valley of flesh between the separate sides of skin flayed open by the cat's claw. Blood falls into dissimilar rivulets dripping like melting wax the length of the wound.

The slash stings but it doesn't feel *that* bad. I don't feel the urge to give a vengeful chase. I've never been big on revenge anyway. Why prolong the agony? Of course, I've always been the *instigator*. I don't even know what revenge feels like.

The Boy Scout Camp

I spray disinfectant on the wound while picturing the maniacal look of vengeance on Kris's face when he let go of the cat. I can't help but laugh which takes much of the sting away!

All doctored up, I decide to go to the Boy Scout Camp a couple hundred yards south of the cottage where, hopefully, I'll meet up with one or both of the Peters brothers under the big oak tree where we always meet to chop wood or shoot our BB guns. I grab my army surplus hatchet and head for the screened door. Out back, I'm joined by Gray, our Weimaraner dog, my protector and constant companion.

Gray and I walk across the backyard to a path toward the Boy Scout Camp, through underbrush, dwarf pines, and lake grasses, to a wide-open area of tan-colored sand parallel to the lake protected from strong winds blowing off the Great Lake by a ridge of dunes and weather-beaten pines stretching the length of The Point. Here, for two weeks each summer, a couple busloads of Boy Scouts from the Detroit area pitch pup tents, drink bug juice, go on nature hikes, braid plastic strips into lanyards, and swim twice a day in the cold glacial water of the Great Lake.

But, neither of the Peters brothers are in sight. Damn! I guess I'll have to chop wood by myself.

While Gray hunts through the trees and underbrush for the scent of any animal she can bark at, I put my green, straight-handled, dull-bladed army surplus hatchet, that constantly loses its wedge, to work.

The Raft

The old hatchet is not good for much other than smashing wood apart. I smash fallen pine branches and struggle in vain to chop through the harder oak limbs. It's a pretty good hammer though. I use it to nail together the raft I'm making from wood I find washed up along the shoreline.

Soon I grow tired of smashing wood by myself so I decide to look for usable lumber washed up onshore that I can use for the floorboards of the raft.

Gray and I walk east toward the Great Lake, past the scrub pines and over the high windbreaker dunes I mentioned earlier. We move across a wide tan-colored beach to the shoreline of the Great Lake.

Gray Plays/I Call it a Day

While I search along the beach for washed-up boards, Gray frolics in the water, sprinting back and forth. Picking up a piece of driftwood, she barks at me, then runs away, looking over her shoulder, hoping I'll try to catch her and we'll have a tug-of-war battle over ownership of the wood she found.

I search for a quarter mile in both directions. But on this day, the beach is clear of anything useful.

Disappointed, I decide to call it a day. Hatchet in hand, Gray and I head back to the cottage along the same path we took going out.

Back at the Cottage

Back at the cottage, the position of the sun tells me it's barely mid-afternoon. So Gray and I decide to take a swim.

We walk along the west side of the cottage, across the front yard, then turn right at the path leading to the beach, a short distance up a slight incline, then down across a wide tan-colored beach. I come face to face with my brother emerging from the water, his shivering lips dark purple from swimming too long in cold Great Lake water.

A Grim Face I'm Not Familiar With

Entering the water, Kris and I come face-to-face. I'm having strange feelings never felt before. It feels like I'm being forced to wear a grim face I'm very much not familiar with. Kris smiles, the left side of his mouth pulled back in a sly grin, looking up at me through the tops of his eyes.

What does the look on his face mean? He's laughing at me! Is this what it feels like to be laughed at? I've never been laughed at before. Is this how people feel when they are teased and taunted, unable to fight back?

I lower my head. I'm feeling alone. An empty feeling like suddenly something about life is missing or I've lost something. I feel alone.

Just Before My First Dive

Ten or fifteen yards offshore, in stomach-deep water, just before taking my first dive, I turn to see if Kris is still there or what he's doing. To my surprise, he's facing me, his feet half covered with sand, lake water washing over them, hands on his hips, a towel over his head and shoulders. He's stopped shivering. He wears the same sly smile on his face like he knows something I don't.

I realize the source of my feelings. "He outsmarted me!" So that's what I'm feeling! I'm not smart! I was unable to fend for myself. I feel powerless, sad, and worthless. Ashamed for the countless times I've given Kris the same feelings.

Images of the crazy cat and the v-shaped wound dripping blood appear in my mind. Feeling like a fool, I decide to yell friendly words at Kris but words fail me. His eyes are boring a hole through me. My brain is a blank. So, I wait with great trepidation unable to do anything until he decides what's next.

What's Next?

Catching me by surprise, he points his finger at me, throws his head back and begins cackling and whooping with laughter at the sky, making fun of me. "You should have seen your face!" he says, his voice in mocking, soprano range, "Now you know what it feels like. HA HA HA HA HA… ."

He turns away. My eyes are glued to him, unblinking, waiting, hoping he'll go away and leave me alone. While walking away, his back toward me, he raises his arm and flips me the bird while shaking his head side-to-side, sounding like a laughing hyena.

I feel terrible. Downtrodden. Is this how people feel when they've been teased unrelentingly?

At the top of the dune, he turns, and one last time (while I watch feeling dumbfounded) he points at me, throws his head back cackling loudly at the sky or anyone within a hundred yards who can hear. Bent at the waist, he's laughing so hard he can't stop. I close my eyes briefly, moving my head from left-to-right. When I open them, he's gone.

Dropping Straight Down/Hot Feelings

I drop straight down into sixty-five-degree Great Lake water. The Lake's pure water cools the smoldering fire inside my brain. Cold water and the silence of being submerged envelope me. My hot feelings of fear and confusion slowly lessen their dissonance. I'm submerged in a world of peace and quietude. I roll into a ball and free float, the sound of waves whispering off in the distance.

Once again, I feel like I'm part of another world within the Great Lake, apart from the complicated world of human transgressions. Soon my mind quiets. My embarrassment replaced by a sense of calm acceptance.

When it's time to rise up, I touch the bottom, feeling the ridge-like sand waves beneath my toes, their forms miniature reflections from the movement of waves above.

Rising from the water, a gusting breeze makes goosebumps along my arms. When I open my eyes, a vision of Kris's laughing face appears in my mind, while at the same time, new feelings of respect and admiration well up inside. Such feelings of respect and admiration, I never even knew existed for another person.

I never felt the same about my brother after that day.

Autumn

Outside My Fifth-Grade Window

Prelude

The gray morning sky does not dampen
my sunny disposition this first day of Fifth!
The brilliant, light-filled days of summer are not
distant memories, hidden below the surface.

No, they're easy scratchings
to fill daydreams
if I want to relive an adventure.

I feel comfortably trapped between two illusory worlds;
past dreams of life on the Great Lake and
a whirlpool of expectant dreams
waiting
to be
lived.

The Elm Tree

From my seat in the middle of the first row, I steal a little time each day to gaze through windows running the length of my fifth-grade classroom at a meadow of brown, field grass beyond the playground in back of the school. A hundred yards beyond the playground, up a gentle rise, a giant elm tree spreads its limbs wide over the open field.

A quarter mile past the elm, cars appear as small boxes, slowly moving left-to-right, right-to-left across the thin gray edge of the two-lane concrete Highway M-78 that connects my little town to the rest of the world.

The year? 1957.

Acres of Farmland Changing Color

Beyond the highway, acres of farmland stretch to the horizon over gentle hills. The fields change color with the different growing seasons, green corn knee-high by the Fourth of July

41

and winter wheat in spring. Golden-yellow wheat by mid-summer. The corn turns yellow in late summer and fall.

Red barns and farm houses appear as tiny silhouettes. Tractors plowing or reaping seem to barely move. Horizontal lines of windbreaker trees separate fields. Snow lines in the fallow fields point north scattering the panorama. After corn is harvested, the land lies fallow, void of anything living.

The field grass beyond the playground moves in circular patterns, sometimes lying flat before swirling in the opposite direction, pushed and shoved by the north wind from beyond the Arctic Circle. The steady drop in temperature is a signal telling every living thing it's time to prepare for the long, cold night of winter sleep. The soil becomes dormant; resting along with every other living thing.

Late Fall/Early Winter

It's cold outside now. At least half of the orange, red, and yellow leaves have dropped from the trees. The smell of leaves burning in the streets around town is a calming incense creating pleasant memories for a ten-year-old: drives in the country with all four windows open, past the fields and woods, campfires at the cottage, or night games under the lights, watching the courting rituals of the big kids at the games, or peeping at them making out at the movie theatre downtown on Friday night where everyone goes between athletic seasons.

As the temperature drops, instead of the light, zippered jacket worn during Indian summer, I'll wear a thermal t-shirt under a flannel shirt, a crew neck sweater, my heavy coat with a buckle on the front and a stocking cap. It's my winter attire along my three-block trek to school or after school when I might be shoveling walks, sledding, ice skating, having snowball fights, throwing snowballs at cars, or just horsing around.

Letting my Mind Wander: What Would it Be?

When I'm not filling in answers to questions in language, or reading workbooks, or doing rows of arithmetic problems (two- or three-story problems at the bottom of each page), I dream about the world of plants and trees and animals in the world beyond the playground in back of my school.

What would it be like to sleep all winter inside a tunnel of grass or spend winter inside a one-room cottage carved from the inside of the giant elm, *like pictures I've seen in stories illustrated by Beatrice Potter,* protected by the curved walls of the elm behind a thick wooden door with brass hinges, a door handle, and a big brass lock? A small fire casts a friendly yellow glow into the room where a male and female field mouse sit across from each other at a roughly-hewn table and chairs holding cups of hot tea. Through a four-pane window next to the thick door, white puff balls of snow are falling. The female field mouse has a humorous look on her face. Both paws are raised. One finger points upward. She's telling a funny story about an incident she experienced over the summer.

Blowing Sideways

The male field mouse listens with a smile on his face, both hands encircling his cup. Steam curls its way up from both cups. Outside the four-pane window, snow blows sideways in streaks of white lines. Wind blowing across window panes creates three-note chords that rise and fall like moans of a diesel engine pulling a train.

But the mice are safe and warm inside the tree.

The stories they tell each other are filled with great detail. So much commonality that each is transported back in time as they relive each other's experiences as if in real time.

Such is the nature of dreams in the animal world during hibernation.

The Field Mouse

The cold north wind blowing hard against the windows running the length of my classroom makes me wonder; how does a tiny field mouse stay warm all winter if it doesn't have a safe comfortable tree to live in?

The field mouse uses blades of dead field grass precisely cut with her teeth. For added warmth, she weaves the feathers, newspaper, and grass together making a flat, woven blanket.

Gripping it with her claws, she wraps herself inside the insulated grass and feather cocoon to be warm all winter.

The Warmth of a Beating Heart

During coldest winter nights when the sky is crystal clear and there is no wind, the field mouse lies curled around the warmth of its beating heart. A layer of fat collected over the summer, the feather-grass quilt, the blades of field grass lying flat with snow create layers of insulation.

The boy stares out across a wide field of grass picturing what it would be like to be a mouse sleeping in a field of grass burrowed inside a quilt of feathers and cut grass.

The mouse, in twilight sleep, sees the sky above as a wide field of grass. A boy's face appears in the distance.

While the boy wonders if what he is seeing is real, the field mouse dreams. And in her dream, she sees the boy's face looking down with a look of wonder.

The Eternal Mystery

Great Lake Pounds the Shoreline with Fury

The only word
to describe the rushing sound
of one continual line of whitecaps
breaking parallel to the shore,
a half mile in each direction.
Extraordinary!

Approaching surges
mirrored along the horizon line
crackle with fluid electricity.
Waves reaching their peak
six-, eight-, ten-feet tall
begin their descent,
fingers reaching downward
into the swale below,
are drawn up and over
by their own weight.

Wide and round and fat,
they break along their curvature
wrapped around air
trapped inside the curl,
streaks of gray and white
and filigrees of sandy green,
rolling forward and down,
white foam coursing the front,
passion spent,
collapsed onto sand
flowing through
the sieve of past conversions
the clock of time
along the hour-glass shoreline
each grain a tiny piece
of what was once
a mighty seed, the earth's crust
when time had
just begun.

Journey to Marquette

Anxious to begin my journey from Durand at the center of Michigan's Lower Peninsula to Marquette four-hundred miles north in the Upper Peninsula to visit my favorite high school football coach, I grab my sleeping bag, shove three roast beef sandwiches, two Yoo-Hoos, underwear and socks, a sweatshirt, and my little transistor radio into my backpack.

After saying goodbye to Mom and Dad, I head out the back door, cut across the field in back of our house, past the back of the bowling alley to M-78 where I stick out my thumb, catch a ride to Owosso in record time, then head north on M-27, back in 1963 when I was fifteen.

I sleep under an elm tree in a farmer's field the first night outside the little town of Chesaning, the air cool and breezy, the sky crystal clear, where I eat a roast beef sandwich and sip a Yoo-Hoo while gazing up at the stars through elm leaves, listening to the Motown sounds of CKLW-AM radio out of Detroit, falling asleep around nine thirty.

Early next morning, I see plenty of families in Chevy Nomads heading north on M-27, branching west to Traverse City or east to Tawas or Oscoda for autumn colors or one last dip in cold Great Lakes' water before school starts after Labor Day.

Riding the Ferry

By noon, I'm on the upper deck of the ferry crossing the Straights of Mackinaw watching the Grand Hotel on Mackinaw Island in the distance with its magnificent white front porch (the longest front porch in the world) and Fort Mackinaw at the highest point of Mackinaw Island, before docking at St. Ignace, the southernmost city in the Upper Peninsula.

Horseflies

A quick ride from St. Ignace leaves me stranded in the middle of the Hiawatha National Forest where for forty-five minutes, I'm bombarded by huge horseflies before a semi-truck driver picks me up and drops me off not far from downtown Marquette, where, after asking around, I learn my coach's house is only a few blocks away.

With high hopes, I knock on the door thinking when he sees me, I'll be welcomed with open arms.

I'm not.

Disappointment

After an uncomfortable silence, we sit on the front steps drinking lemonade, talking about the night we defeated Fenton, our school rival, in the final fifteen seconds of the game. I could tell by the look on his face, I wasn't going to get an invitation for dinner. So I made up an excuse to leave and said goodbye.

Walking away, I realize I've lost all respect for the man. He's no better than most people I've met during my fifteen years of life.

Meatloaf and Girly Mags

That night I pay $3.50 for a meatloaf dinner downtown, a nickel for a pack of Juicy Fruit gum at the drugstore on the corner next door. Then, for some crazy reason, steal a girly magazine from a rack just inside the front door coming a hair's breath away from getting caught by the druggist who followed me out of the drugstore and watched me cross the street.

I didn't like the way I felt after stealing the magazine. So I figure now that I know what it feels like to be a thief, I don't have to steal anything ever again.

I spend the night in a small city park behind an oak tree next to a statue of Father Marquette where I read my girly magazine with Pere Marquette looking over my shoulder, falling asleep around eleven o'clock.

Little GTO

Early next morning, I wash up at the restaurant, eat two breakfasts, grab my gear, walk a couple blocks, and stick out my thumb on M-23. In short order, a maniacal-looking mechanic with black fingernails wearing greasy bib overalls driving a souped-up GTO with four-on-the-floor and a big tachometer on the steering column slows down and asks if I want a ride.

At speeds up to 120 mph, we arrive at St. Ignace in half the time it took to travel the opposite direction. By nine o'clock, I'm crossing the Straights of Mackinaw heading south toward Mackinaw City, the northernmost city in Michigan's Lower Peninsula.

Fort Mackinaw and the Red Coats

While dozing on the top deck of the ferry, a cool breeze off Lake Huron brings with it visions of cannon fire raining down on the Red Coats from high atop Mackinaw Island during the Revolutionary War when battles were fought for control of the shipping lanes through the Straights.

The ferry's powerful engines surging in reverse wake me from my reverie as we dock at Mackinaw City.

Hitching the Coastline

Rides south on M-23 along the Lake Huron shoreline past Rogers City, through Alpena, Harrisville, and Oscoda are plentiful but only for short distances.

Around nightfall, I arrive in East Tawas where in the early 1900s, my great grandparents built a tiny cottage on the shoreline of Lake Huron on Tawas Point near the Coast Guard Station. Years later, my brother and I were fortunate to spend three idyllic summers exploring the virgin land and lakes of The Point. The U.S. Government sold the land to the State of Michigan in 1959. Now it is a state park.

In Jail for the Night

Anyway, I'm tired and hungry, and it's almost dark, so I decide, *What the heck, I'll ask if I can sleep in a jail cell at the newly-constructed Justice Center in East Tawas.*

Inside the station, I tell the officers my name. I tell them I'm returning from an eight-hundred-mile journey to Marquette and back to see my favorite football coach. They listen patiently with friendly smiles. Then I drop the bomb.

"So, I was wondering, since it's almost dark and I don't have any place to stay, do you mind if I sleep in an empty cell?"

After the laughter and backslapping die down, the jail matron, wearing a khaki uniform and a gold badge, ushers me into the first cell on the right.

"All the cells are empty," she tells me. "If anyone is sent to jail tonight, you must leave immediately."

I agree, of course.

The jail matron asks if I'm hungry, which of course, I am. There must have been something about my demeanor that told her I was close to being famished.

To my surprise, she returns with a tray piled high with roast beef, mashed potatoes, green beans, two slices of bread and butter, and two cartons of milk.

I'm too flabbergasted to speak. I think *this is the best thing that has happened to me all day!*

She's a cute girl in her early twenties. She tells me where to put my tray when I'm finished. Staring at the food piled high, I hear myself say, "This is the best thing that's happened to me all day." She smiles at me warmly.

She chooses the right key from around a hundred and fifty attached to her belt. While searching, my eyes gaze at her profile. The left side of her face reminds me of Sandra Dee. She has a slender, almost boyish, figure. After locking the door, she faces me wearing the sweetest smile I've ever seen.

I'm captivated by her sweet face. I can't take my eyes away in expectation of something yet to happen. Before disappearing behind the big door, she turns her head. She gives me a second dose of her pretty, smiling face. This time with white teeth showing. She turns and vanishes behind a thick steel door.

I'm left standing alone staring at the cell door wondering if she saw me go slack-jawed when she smiled.

I eat ravenously. After dinner, I collapse on a cot. Despite the bright lights shining all night, I instantly fall asleep and stay that way until morning.

The Sound of Jangling Keys

Next morning around six-thirty, I wake to the sound of jangling keys and a tray piled high with scrambled eggs, hash-brown potatoes, and two cartons of milk. After breakfast, I wash up and brush my teeth in the tiny sink inside the cell.

Anxious to continue my journey, I begin wondering when they'll let me out. I don't know how to notify the jail matron. So, for the heck of it, I rake my metal cup back and forth a few times (very gently, of course) across the metal bars like I've seen in prison movies.

Whatever I did must have worked. We were both laughing when she came through the big iron door to let me out.

After saying goodbye and thanking all my jailhouse friends (especially the jail matron!), I'm back on U.S. Route 23 walking the hitchhiker's walk backwards, facing traffic, my right thumb extended, heading south toward Saginaw through Augres, Omer, and Standish. With any luck, I'll be home before nightfall.

I get lucky.

Two Guys and a Buck

Two guys with a twelve-point buck strapped to the top of their Chevy Impala drive me down M-52 to The Outpost in Standish where I buy lunch for us: foot-long coneys, fries, and Cokes.

Shortly after lunch, we continue a short distance past Deer Acres Roadside Zoo. This is ironic since, at the beginning of summer, we stopped there to pet the tame deer. Now, the car I'm riding in has a gutted deer (looking like it's being choked, its flaccid tongue blowing in the breeze) strapped to the roof of the car. But I don't say anything.

Later, passing through Saginaw while stopped at a red light in front of huge Victorian-style houses built by the lumber barons at the turn of the century, I smile remembering an experience we had as a family last year returning from the cottage at the end of the summer. We were stopped at the same light when Gray jumped out of the rear window to chase a dog barking at us from the car next to ours.

Body by Fisher

Forty minutes later, I'm standing on M-78 at Lennon Corners, not far from Durand, watching the white tail of the gutted buck recede toward Swartz Creek, five miles in the opposite direction I'm headed.

I don't have long to wait. A couple of guys who were older, big kids who graduated a few years ago from the same school I go to, pick me up on their way home from working first shift at the General Motors Fischer Body Plant in Flint. Twenty minutes later, they drop me off at my doorstep.

I slip inside the side door through the screened-in porch but almost immediately run into Dad who asks me if I've gotten around to mowing the empty lot next door. I'm speechless. Turning and walking away, I feel empty inside. He doesn't seem to realize, or care, that I've just returned from an eight-hundred-mile journey to Marquette and back. Doesn't he know I've been gone for three nights and four days? It's as if my time away had been snipped from a reel of film. Like I hadn't even been gone.

That evening, seated around the dinner table, they ask me a few questions. What did I think of the trip across the Straights of Mackinaw? Or, did I have to wait very long for rides? But nothing very pertinent. Then, before I can even tell them about spending the night in the Tawas jail, they apologize and leave for some special event.

Adding insult to injury, Mom asks me to clear off the table and wash the dinner dishes.

That Night in Bed

That night in bed, I feel restless. Unable to sleep. Doubly frustrated.

First, they didn't seem to care anything about the adventures I had on my eight-hundred-mile journey. It doesn't seem they know I'd been gone three nights and four days!

Second, from my bed upstairs inside the alcove created by a dormer window, I wanted to watch a spectacular full moon slowly move across the night sky. But it is nowhere in sight. It has already passed overhead.

I wonder what it would be like to be under the big elm tree in the field in the back of our house looking up through fall leaves at a night sky listening to Motown Music on CKLW AM radio out of Detroit?

Drifting into sleep, I dream of a full moon against deep blue space, the stars like snowflakes waiting to fall from the sky.

Tawas Point
Full-Moon Night

Descent to Band Outcast

The percussion section in the back left corner of our tiny band room is cordoned off from the rest of the band by a bass drum, three snare drums, three timpani drums, a set of chimes, a full-sized gong, and a silver glockenspiel on a stand.

Most days, the band director, Mr. Granville Stuart, who we call Mr. S, works with different instrumental sections. We, in the percussion section, wait to play. Near the end of the period, to appease the percussion section, we play a couple marches.

Out of boredom, my ADD aversion to sitting still and having free time, I visit vantage points hidden from Mr. S's gaze. I flirt with a couple of girls or read lips, laugh at dumb things happening, or watch with sympathy while Mr. S, his angry face bright red, his pock-marked-chipmunk cheeks puffed out, his words cutting and sharp, humiliating various band members unable to play their parts perfectly, haranguing them to practice more, questioning their commitment.

I can move around in the back as long as I don't interfere with his teaching, which eventually is how I begin my slow descent from first chair drummer to band outcast.

Anger Multiplied

My descent to outcast status isn't because I have the freedom to move around. It's what I carry in my hands and what I **do** with my hands while carrying around a pair of 2B drum sticks. I keep them in constant motion against the side of my leg, slapping out the rhythms to Motown or rock songs that constantly flow through my brain. Inevitably, the tips of my flailing sticks click against each other, or tap a music stand, or worse, one or both sticks slip between my fingers, fall, and tap out their own syncopated beats against the wood floor as if played by puppet strings.

Which infuriates Mr. S!

Mr. S's anger intensifies with each incident. Eventually, if I make even the slightest sound, he lashes out at me; his chipmunk cheeks and pock-marked skin reddening, at times bordering on purple. By and by, his rants increase in duration, sometimes lasting two or three minutes!

One day in the middle of one of his tirades, a purple vein, the size of a pencil, appears beneath the skin of his forehead!

High Theatre/Comic Relief

Eventually, the clash between my clumsiness and Mr. S's temper become high theatre. My bandmates start to look forward with great expectation to unexpected noises from the percussion section not just for the entertainment value, but as the duration of his tirades grow, they don't have to worry about being called on to play as often.

Without realizing it, I had become a scapegoat. Or, maybe, their comic relief?

As Mr. S's tirades increase in length and intensity, I start to take his threats to kick me out more seriously. I don't want to get kicked out of band! I love band! Where else can a person go to listen to live music every day? So I make an agreement with myself **not** to touch my sticks until it's time to play, which means I'll have to leave them alone for at least forty minutes every day. A pretty tall order.

Surprisingly, things go pretty well. For a while anyway.

Starving Lovers

As time wears on, the temptation to pick up my sticks and wail on the side of my leg grows stronger. Like a couple of starving lovers, my hands and my drum sticks yearn for our mutual embrace.

One day, after hearing Marvin Gaye and Tammy Terrell sing *Ain't No Mountain High Enough*, I'm inspired. The song keeps rolling through my head until I can't resist the urge to play along. I grab my sticks, groove along with the beat for a while, then gently put them back into their little cubby where they belong.

Man! It felt *great* to play along with those Motown beats!

After the Marvin and Tammy incident, I keep pushing the limit as I listen to my internal music for longer periods of time. Eventually, I realize I've fallen off the (band) wagon.

Realizing I can't resist the temptation to wail away against my leg, I make a formal pact with myself. *I will grip my sticks tightly, avoid anything solid, and most of all, pay attention to what I'm doing!*

Things go pretty well for a while. I've imposed a modicum of restraint upon myself, a happy medium between wailing against my leg and gently laying my sticks down, when I find myself getting carried away.

Little do I know.

Going Out with a Bang

Oddly, the incident that brings about my demise is not the result of something I do out of carelessness or lack of awareness. There had always been bad blood between Mr. S and me. Maybe getting the boot was inevitable. It could have happened any day for any number of reasons large or small.

When it finally **does** happen, at least I have the satisfaction of knowing I went out with a bang!

Here's how it happened.

The *Anvil Chorus*

One ordinary day, I walk back to the percussion section where I'm greeted by the sight of a three-hundred-and-fifty-pound blacksmith's anvil perched on a flimsy-looking table leaning against the back wall of the already-cramped quarters of the percussion section.

An anvil in the drum section? What the hell is that all about?

Second chair drummer Carlton Bischoff shows me a ballpeen hammer which he explains, "We'll be using this to play the anvil when the band performs the *Anvil Chorus* at the annual Easter Concert."

Hmmm, I wonder. *How can Mr. S possibly think a three-hundred-and-fifty-pound anvil sitting on a flimsy-looking table can produce a musical tone when struck by a heavy ballpeen hammer?*

Later I'm flabbergasted to learn for some strange reason, Mr. S chooses **me** to play the anvil which turns out to probably be one of the biggest mistakes of his life.

A Disaster Looking for a Place to Happen

The first time we rehearse the *Anvil Chorus*, I slam the ballpeen hammer against the anvil with such force that for one brief moment it feels like I've morphed into a real blacksmith! Naturally there's no ringing vibration, therefore no musical tone.

Instead, the heavy hammer striking three-hundred-and-fifty pounds of solid steel creates a resounding **thud** that's heard in the corners of every room throughout the entire three-story school.

My friend in study hall, one floor up at the opposite end of the school, jokingly told me a couple of his friends thought they were feeling the rumblings of an earthquake.

My band mates stop playing, looking dumbfounded. Since they *know* the source of the rumble, they begin laughing hysterically. While everyone laughs, I happen to look down at the leg of the flimsy table.

What I see is a disaster about to happen!

Below the din of laughter, you could have heard me mutter, "Oh shit! That son of a bitch is gonna go!"

At this point, the dominoes begin falling.

I Do Not Want This to Happen!

The anvil seems magnetically drawn to the left-front corner of the flimsy table where the leg is buckling inward at an alarming rate. As the leg buckles, the anvil picks up speed, moving closer and closer to the edge.

I picture the anvil slipping over the edge causing a **sonic boom** with collateral damage to the floor, all of which I **know** I'll get the blame for. I do **not** want this to happen!

In a desperate attempt to stop its forward motion, I grab the edge of the table, pull up with all my strength while picturing how pissed off Mr. S is going to be when it drops. It's depressing because I know I'm only postponing the inevitable.

Since that day I've wondered how people can possibly know how difficult it can be to convince a three-hundred-and-fifty-pound anvil to stop moving after it has made up its mind it wants to head south?

It's not difficult. It's impossible!

When the futility of my efforts become obvious, I let go, jump back, and watch helplessly as the tapered end of the anvil drops over the edge, picks up three feet of speed, strikes the floor, stabbing itself between the butted ends of two wood strips of flooring.

When the back half of the anvil comes to rest, an eight-foot strip of vintage pinewood flooring pops up and splinters down the middle with a loud crack!

I jump back as the anvil falls, but I guess a little too forcefully?

Chimes to the Left of Me, Tubas to the Right

I feel something heavy graze my shoulder. I turn just in time to see a set of brass chimes arching toward second-chair-tuba player Danny Dunn. Several of the larger chimes land full force onto his right knee, then tumble to the floor, intensifying the already crazy disharmony in the increasing chaos.

Beneath the sound of the bells, bells, bells, you could hear poor Danny howl, howl, howling with pain.

Instinctively, Danny rises but with only one leg supporting his weight, the inertia of the tuba's heavy bell pulls him out of his chair. The bell continues its forward momentum, grazing first-chair-trumpet player Ace Cooper's cheek before coming to rest on his thighs and the thighs of second-chair-trumpet player Richie Sutton.

Richie's fight or flight instincts immediately kick into high gear. He jerks his body so violently to the left that the bell of his trumpet strikes Geraldine Bunt's prized new cornet bending the second valve.

Geraldine is a farm girl who has no problem expressing her feelings with colorful language. "You son of a bitch," she yells. Then, suddenly for some reason I'll never know, Geraldine's new cornet takes flight.

I watch the shiny cornet float through the air in slow motion toward first-chair-baritone player Eddy Beker's head! The mouthpiece deflects off Eddy's forehead. It starts to bleed in unison with the cornet striking the pinewood floor.

Blood Feud

For a split second, the room gets really quiet as everyone contemplates the trickle of blood curling around Eddy's eye. Eddy smears blood all over his cheek, then looks at the tips of his fingers. The sight of blood startles him. "What the … ?"

Dazed and confused, therefore not paying attention to what he's doing, Eddy stands and wheels to the left. The bottom of the baritone grazes his music stand sending it forward against the back of Candy Higgins's chair. The music stand barely misses Candy's nose as she had turned her head to see what the commotion was behind her.

Candy reaches beneath her chair. She grabs a spiral notebook and rolls it into a tube. She has had a running feud with Eddy Beker for some time.

"I'm going to beat the crap out of you, Eddy Beker!" she hollers while standing.

Candy rises so forcefully that the bassoon, resting cross ways on her lap, flips forward at an oblique angle. The double reed slashes across the back of flute player Marian Beezner's chair, barely missing her shoulder.

Full Moon Rising

Marian, a sensitive girl prone to overreacting and easily brought to tears, overreacts. She jumps up so forcefully that the piccolo on her lap slips down the incline of her skirt, pinwheels across the floor, disappearing beneath first-chair-clarinet player Nan Hunter's chair.

Nan's eyes and the spinning piccolo move in perfect unison.

In her zeal to retrieve the piccolo, Nan reaches so far under her chair that her butt rises off her seat while it appears her head has completely disappeared between her knees!

The Flying White Dot

I'm watching all these events unfold behind the timpani drums at the back of the room directly in line with Mr. S's podium. I'm feeling utterly helpless to stop the increasing chaos. Suddenly, a tiny white dot appears. The dot keeps growing larger. When it zips past my left ear, I realize Mr. S has thrown his baton at me!

Strange as it seems, I momentarily picture myself wearing a black eye patch while Mr. S, a look of despair on his face, pleads with the school board to keep his job.

When Mr. S steps off the podium to come after me, his fingers curled waist high like he's carrying an invisible basketball, Nan's head rises from between her knees. Already dizzy from rising up too quickly, she sees the crazed look on Mr. S's face, his fingers poised to strangle me. Her eyes become as Dad would say, "The size of a couple of horse turds!"

Nan's so startled she slips off the side of her chair sending it careening toward two snare drums and the big bass drum.

I hear crashing sounds with deep undertones.

While Mr. S struggles to squeeze between a timpani drum and the glockenspiel, I decide it's time to make my escape.

Carnage

I'm stepping sideways toward the band-room door in the narrow space between the last row of the clarinet section and my back against the wall. Poised to open the door, my fist wrapped tightly around the handle, I take a moment to survey the carnage.

Danny Dunn, the tuba player, grimaces in pain while rubbing both knees. Geraldine Bunt continues to harangue Richie Sutton holding her cornet inches from his face. It sounds like she's calling Richie a "chicken plucker" or maybe it was a "sock sucker?"

With both hands covering her face, Marian Beemer is bouncing up and down sobbing while Nan Hunter, lying on her right side, holds the piccolo high for all to see, wearing a triumphant grin, her skirt a good foot above her knees, a hair's breadth away from exposing herself to the entire class.

Then, there's Mr. S moving toward me, crouched low, arms and fingers extended, his face beet red, the pulsing vein in the middle of his forehead bulged out like a finger grown beneath his skin, his chipmunk cheeks puffing in and out like a pair of mini bellows, his jaw pushed forward, the bottom row of his teeth visible, his face given vicious proportion by the maniacal look in his eyes.

In a last-ditch effort to defend myself, I shout, "But it wasn't my fault!"

But Mr. S is beyond reason. So I make my escape slamming the door shut behind me.

Pirouetting Principal/Full Body Block

When I wheel around, the school principal, an old schoolmarm who had been Dad's principal, pirouettes away from me. To my dismay, I realize I've just thrown a full-body block into her. I'm thinking *if my block turns into a tackle, I'm in deep shit.* Luckily, she regains her balance by grabbing the edge of a table.

Our eyes slowly focus on each other. She slowly moves her head from side to side, the left half of her mouth pulled into a sardonic half smile. "Just like your father," she whispers in a voice only I can hear. Her eyes become stone cold, narrowing into horizontal slits as they lock onto mine.

Barely audible she says, "See me in the morning."

I nod my head in acknowledgment.

Turning, she takes three steps and stops. With her face half in profile, she says, "*Early* tomorrow morning!" And walks away.

Next morning an hour before school, Miss Crane and I have our pow-wow. I tell her about the anvil and the flimsy table and the ensuing chaos. Her face is placid, unblinking. I tell her I love being in the band. She slowly nods her head, her eyes boring into mine not saying a word. I look down, then to my surprise, I hear myself say, with a contrite tone, "Maybe I'm growing so fast I forget where the end of my fingers are from one week to the next."

Sensing my regret by this act of unconscious honesty, she accepts my explanation.

Next, we discuss the terms of my punishment.

I'm out of band class for the next week. I'll spend an hour after school which raises hell with being at football practice. With further deliberation between Miss Crane, the coach, and me, we make a deal. I'm to run ten laps in full pads, including my helmet, around the big field **after** practice each night for a week.

A week later, I'm back in band, minding my Ps and Qs in better physical condition than anyone in the entire school.

Entering the room, I take a seat where the flimsy table with the anvil used to reside behind the timpani drums next to the glockenspiel and the big brass chimes thinking, *Gosh, it feels great to be back in band. I mean, where else can you go every day and hear live music?*

The Runner

The runner catches the punt at the thirty-five-yard line in front of the home-team bleachers, takes two steps backward, tucks the ball into the crook of his arm, lowers his right shoulder, and begins running a looping arc toward the opposite side of the field. I wait at the forty-five-yard line in front of the opposing team's bleachers.

I feel a collective sense of awareness from the visiting fans as we both realize the runner and I are on a collision course.

I take a wide stance, lower my butt, curl my hands into loose fists. Rocking side-to-side on the balls of my feet, I watch, anxious for the runner to arrive. A soft voice inside my brain whispers, *You will **not** let this son of a bitch get past you.* I know that he knows we will soon make violent contact. I smile.

Predatory

My heart and lungs pump a sense of rage into the center of my brain. I feel like a predator about to pounce on its prey. Eager to feel the pain, I picture the runner's helmet split down the middle like a pumpkin dropped from a two-story building. Fifteen yards from where I wait, I spread my arms as if to embrace the runner.

My legs become coiled springs that I will unleash at precisely the right moment to stop the runner in his tracks, to drive him into the ground!

I narrow my field of vision, focusing on my target, the area below the sternum where both sides of his rib cage meet just below the heart. A split second before contact I see the top half of the number on the runner's jersey, the outline of his helmet against the lights of the scoreboard, his head barely lowered, eyes wide with fear.

At precisely the right moment, I unleash the coiled power of my legs.

The Tackle

I feel my body spring forward. My left shoulder sinks into the soft spot below the runner's rib cage. With my left arm wrapped around his back, my hand clenched into a fist, I pull the runner tightly into my grasp, hearing a forceful "Whoof!" as the air is forced from his lungs.

With the runner held tightly, I open my eyes. Green grass, a clod of dirt, part of the white chalk line, the numbers on the scoreboard blur across my field of vision.

While pulling him more closely, I use my right arm to lift him off his feet. Driving forward and down with the help of gravity, I complete the full ninety-degree arc of the tackle, sending the runner crashing to the ground.

That Desperate Sucking Noise

I hear the clatter of shoulder pads, the dull thud of the runner's helmet bouncing off the turf, then that desperate honking sound people make when all air has been forced from their lungs and they can't catch a breath. For a brief moment, they think they're going to suffocate.

I lay partially on the runner, listening to him struggle to breathe, familiar with his momentary sense of desperation, knowing that within a few seconds, he'll realize he's not going to die.

Adding insult to injury, I place my right hand against the runner's chest and push myself into a standing position before returning to the bench.

A Persistent Sound

My mind is empty of thought, but a persistent sound draws my attention to the left toward the opposing-team's bleachers. When I turn to look at the spectators, I am astonished at the looks on their faces.

Many of the opposing-team's fans are standing, clapping their hands, their eyes fixed on where I stand, wearing smiles of respect or wide-eyed wonder.

Burning Leaves on a Cool Autumn Night

I turn and trot toward my side of the field. The applause sounds like heavy raindrops splattering against concrete during a summer rainfall.

Each time my cleats sink into the ground, the applause grows softer until, finally, it seems I have emerged from a heavy downpour on a summer day into a cool autumn night, the smell of burning leaves in the air.

Spring

Field Tree
Pinconning, Michigan

Collecting the Sap

Eight giant, old-growth maple trees line the east side of Mackinaw Street between the sidewalk and the curb. Mackinaw Street rises up and ends at Monroe Road. Monroe Road runs left-to-right across the front of our house.

If you walk a straight line from the end of Mackinaw Street across Monroe Road, you'll cross the front yard and find yourself on the front porch of our house. One day while standing on the porch gazing at the eight maple trees lining Mackinaw Street, Dad becomes transfixed by their beauty. By and by, he sees a vision of his two son's faces.

He makes a connection between the trees and his sons. Snapping his fingers, he thinks he has a brilliant idea. *We'll tap those maple trees and make our own maple syrup! I'll break the news to everyone after dinner.*

The Story Begins

After dinner, with his friendliest salesman face, he tells us he has plans for a family project. My brother and I roll our eyes at each other.

"We're going to tap the maple trees along Mackinaw. We'll make our own maple syrup, maple candy, and maple fudge. And we'll learn a lot in the process."

He's not asking us if we want to **do** the project. He's telling us we **will**. We will collect the sap in a big jug twice a day at four a.m. and six p.m. My brother and I will carry a jug big enough to hold the sap from all eight trees. The spout makes it easy to pour the sap into an iron cauldron where we will be cooking it at a slow boil.

He keeps telling us how interesting it will be. He's got that Mr. Wizard look in his eyes. He's giving us the science of transforming maple sap into syrup.

He tells us the most important job will be keeping an eye on the cooking sap. It takes constant vigilance to keep the temperature in the range of simmering and a slow boil.

If the sap rises to a high boil, the heat must be turned down quickly or the sap will burn. One person falling down on the job could mean failure for the whole project.

I'm eager to get started. It **does** sound like it could be fun even though I'll have to rise and shine at four o'clock several times a week.

Tomorrow, we'll take the first step.

Tapping the Trees

Dad uses a ten-pound hammer to drive three-inch copper tubes called taps into the base of each tree, four or five feet off the ground. I carry the tin pails we hang on each tap.

Within a minute, we hear the thrum .... thrum .... thrum of clear maple sap dripping out of the copper taps, onto the bottom of the pails.

Every day, for the next several weeks, my brother and I will take turns collecting sap from the eight trees at four a.m. and six p.m. We switch back and forth every other day. We decide between ourselves who gets up at four o'clock on Sunday.

Collecting the Sap: First Day at Four

The four a.m. visits have a huge impact on my thinking. The world at four a.m. is unlike any world I've been in before. Dark and quiet, it seems like I was the only person alive in the whole world.

I never knew such quiet solitude could exist. It was like walking into a dark wall of silence. So quiet you could probably hear a car door slam ten blocks away.

Crossing Monroe to the sidewalk, I hear my felt-lined boots scrunching over school kids' boot prints frozen in slush. It sounds **so loud** against the wall of silence.

Street Lamps and Brief Reflections

I walk the sidewalk past all eight trees to the end of the block carrying the jug I'll use to collect the sap.

Three street lamps, two at each end and one in the middle, throw yellow halos of light on the sidewalk and between the trees. Shadows between each circle of light briefly snuff me into darkness, then back into a halo of light. Sparkling points of light from a half-moon over my left shoulder reflecting off snow crystals follow me along. *Golly,* I think, *I've never seen the moon look like that before.*

At the last tree furthest from the house, I set the big jug on the sidewalk. Then being careful not to spill a drop, I pour the sap from each of the tin pails into the jug. The jug gets heavier with each pailful of sap.

Sometimes I tell the old trees how grateful I am for sharing their sap with me. Every once in a while, I'll pat the tree affectionately with my gloved hand hoping the tree will understand.

By the time I've reached the tree near the house, the big jug weighs three times as much as when I started.

Another Jug into the Cauldron

Crossing Monroe with the heavy jug, I'm being very careful not to spill a single drop of the precious liquid.

I carry the jug across the front yard, around the back, and into the screened-in porch at the east end of our house. Inside the porch, a sliding-glass door opens into the kitchen. A door on the opposite wall leads to the basement. Down the steps to my right is an old gas-fired stove. Six rows of gas jets fuel the blue flames beneath the cauldron holding the steaming sap and refining its flavor.

Breathing the soft maple fragrance, I pour the jug of newly harvested maple sap into the steaming cauldron.

Ummmm. I'm smelling all eight trees at the same time.

Strange Visitors

Sooner or later, we get used to the delicious fragrance. Maybe like everyone else, given enough time, we take things of value for granted. Like, not going to Carnegie Hall when you live in New York. Or never going to the beach when you're only a few miles away.

You could say **we** take the fragrance for granted. Visitors flocking to our house for ridiculous reasons **do not** take the fragrance for granted.

They come to the door and step inside for all kinds of innocuous reasons. They linger just inside the front door, making small talk much to Dad's frustration.

Some people can't seem to breathe enough of the maple-flavored air inside the house. While talking non-stop, they constantly remark about how good it smells. They even take brief sniffs of air without realizing it.

Some people even tried to take the delicious-smelling air home with them!

A couple of men on different occasions, sucked in as much maple-flavored air as they could hold into their lungs. They were trying to capture the fragrance with deep drafts of air drawn in through their noses. Their flushed faces made them look like a couple of red balloons with ears. Boy, they were in a rush to leave.

I pictured them just inside their homes exhaling the heavenly fragrance while making the most God-awful coughing sounds. Then I wonder if they even make it home before the maple air breaks out of their lungs, leaving them bent over in the car seat gasping for air while furiously rolling up the window.

Gosh, what people will do to immerse themselves in the heavenly fragrance and taste of maple sap.

What About the Maple Sap?

Maple sap is one of nature's finest wines. As is maple syrup, nature's finest nectar.

Maple sap is stored in the trees' roots underground during winter. The stored sap is made by the tree during the previous summer. Thousands, or tens of thousands of leaves act as solar panels, soaking up plenty of sunlight during summer needed to make the sap.

The trees make sap because of a partnership they have with sunlight called photosynthesis. Scientists can't explain how photosynthesis works! Converting sunlight into sugar using the green leaves as a manufacturing facility is still a mystery.

Sap flows from the leaves into the limbs and branches, flowing down the trunk into the roots. As the tree grows, so do the roots underground. More root growth accommodates more sap stored. Stored energy fuels more growth when spring rolls around.

When each year's green solar panels have done their job, they turn golden yellow. One at a time, they drop to the earth. Eventually the leaves become soil, further nourishing the tree.

Come late winter and early spring, some beating heart inside the tree pumps sap from below the ground to the end of every branch, limb, and twig. The sugar sap brings buds alive. The buds become green leaves.

The green leaves absorb sunlight. Photosynthesis creates energy. Stored energy fuels new growth next spring.

And the cycle of life continues.

The Heavenly Taste?

If you didn't know it was maple sap, you'd think you were looking at clear, clean water. But the taste? Heavenly.

Taken straight from the tree on a cold winter day, it's clean and clear, cold and fresh, subtle, and refreshing. The sap tastes slightly sweet with a faint woodsy aftertaste. The flavor is subtle and tantalizing. As refreshingly cool to drink on the coldest mornings as cold water on a hot summer day.

Horrifying

One day toward the end of spring, our golden treasure within reach, I went down to the basement and witnessed a horrifying scene. Mom slept too long during one of her afternoon siestas. The maple syrup burned and then acquired a thick, hard skin. A three-inch gash between the center and the inside wall of the cauldron became a pressure-release valve keeping the skin from growing larger.

When I first looked at the conglomeration, the steam beneath was stretching the skin to maximum height. When the skin reached considerable size, the gash on top snapped open. To my surprise, a well-defined jet of steam shot straight up through the gash at a pretty fast rate of speed.

Boy, oh boy! I thought. *There's a lot of pressure going on in there.* The **spout** of steam looked like a well-defined, puffed-up length of a fat, white shoelace.

With no steam support, the mass collapsed onto the congealed sap beneath. The three-inch gash on top came together like a couple of pursed lips tightly sealing the outer layer of the ugly skin.

Soon the skin begins moving again as if being roused from sleep. Now it becomes a real pressure cooker making a big batch of *Sunday Morning Gone Bad Bizarro World Nega-Syrup.*

Then it looks like someone threw a bunch of marbles at it from the inside! Halfway big, it began huffing and puffing like it was running uphill, but I couldn't see any breaks where air could escape.

The skin was coming more alive by the second. I made a connection between the Maple Monster and the geyser I saw at Yellowstone Park one summer.

The longer I looked at the Monstrous Maple Monster, the stronger my impulse to say, "It's alive! It's alive!"

The nectar had been cooked away. What was left? What can be left if all the good is taken away? Only one thing.

Devilish-looking gunk, that's what.

In any case, weeks of work went up in steam that afternoon.

Boy, was Dad mad.

Ghost Trees Wailing at the Wind

A picture could not do justice
to Arctic wind's ferocity
blowing off the Great Lake at constant speed,
unrelenting, bitterly cold.

White caps rushing toward shore,
water, trees, sand, and leaves ...
combined,
shhsssssssssshhhhhing relentlessly.

My hoody inflated into a reverse parachute
pushes me two steps backward.
Dots of rain prick my face.
The occasional snow flake spirals by.
A walk along the shoreline
is out of the question.

I'm forced to retreat to calmer climes
along the road in front of the cottage
where not long ago,
it seemed so cold.

Turning left half a block past the cottage,
I make my way up the Johnson Street hill
to the bike path along M-23.

Turning left onto the bike path
I walk south toward
the Alabaster Pipeline.

Cars on M-23 traveling into or out
of the little town
fly past my right shoulder.

A mile or so past the pipeline,
I return to the top of the hill.
Descending the hill, I hear
the **snap! crack! rip! braaak!!**
of dead ash trees;
the top half of their trunks
broken like sticks,
exposing splintered,
dagger-like teeth pointing skyward
like angry, hissing beasts
released from confinement
within the tree.

The broken trees point skyward
with snarling fury,
the soul of each tree expressing
its pent up frustration,
raging at nature's forces,
unable to express their furiosity
at the plague of beetles
who gave cause to their demise,
long gone now off to greener pastures.
The ash tree's plaintive wails,
their pent-up frustration,
their solitary ghost sounds,
their howls of pain
unheard in their
after lives!

The ash trees wail with silent fury now.
They've become ghost trees wailing at the wind!

Their pain punctuated by
snap! crack!! snap!! snap!!! crack!!!!!

The initial sound of ultimate rot.

Dance of Life

Arctic wind blows northeast across Great Lake's surface.
It's the first nor'easter of the year,
a roaring beast off the lake
forty-miles-an-hour, cold, hard, steady,
piercing, constant.

Wind that feels like grains of sand
blown against your skin twenty-four hours straight!

It blows against the cottage windows,
with five-note tones, diesel horns heralding
the Polar Express or the spooky, wailing sounds
from grade B horror movies.

The slicing wind breaks twigs, branches,
and good-sized limbs off trees.
They drop straight down
or are drawn along by wind's current.

Leaves swimming in the wind, whisked aloft,
blown sidewise, caterwaul 'cross beds
where other leaves are sleeping
each leaf ending flight encircling the ground
to their own final resting place.
Life taken from life given in return.
Wind scattering seeds for trees.
Leaves dreaming soil alive.
Another breath to scatter seeds,
the nor'easter wind tells its stories another year.

The dance of life continues.

Serenity Stolen

Spring has sprung and I know
because yesterday I saw
a bull ant on the floor
by the fireplace.

And, earlier this morning
while writing these words,
a giant black fly b'zzzzzzz'ing by
had invaded my space.

There are gnats and mosquitos
and other tiny things I can't imagine
sharing air that a week ago
floated crystals of lace-like wings,
each a drifting masterpiece floating down
or streaming sidewise
through air
of crystal clarity.

Air that was mine to breathe while witnessing
the beauty of each and every thing
turned black or white,
stripped bare of all distractions.

My life? More complicated now,
avoiding the lines of intersection
between their search
for whatever it is they're searching for
and purest air I've been breathing.

Air I've shared with no one, I now share
with all the little things that come alive
each spring.

The eggs of their existence
frozen in humus or crystalline
within the muck
when trees released their bed covers
to darkest cold intensity.

The soil fecund now.

Warmer sun's return
has freed them
from their amber spaces.

These creatures that
surround me now,
within my sight,
that feed upon my light,
that touch my flesh,
they even share with me my breath,
my choice bereft,
the world no longer stripped bare
of all confusion and complexity,
black and white, clean and fresh!

They've stolen
my serenity!

Life Knowledge

He gave us the freedom to explore
the sandy beaches, dunes, trout streams,
and woods along the shoreline
of the Great Lake

We spent our time swimming in glacial ice,
melted to sixty-five-degree water.
We ran through the pines.
We rode our bikes to places unknown
until we got there.

We were like caged animals allowed to run free,
exploring inland ponds, clubbing frogs,
shooting BB's while camped out
behind windbreaker pines along high dunes,
running the length of Tawas Point
wrapped around Tawas Bay.

We slept next to campfire embers,
facing stars seen through
crystal-clear skies
blown clean by Great Lake's breeze
before drifting into sleep.

I fished alongside the Coast Guard boathouse
at the end of the dock, stretched a hundred yards
into the bay where I caught
perch, smallmouth bass,
or if I was lucky,
a good-sized pike.

He taught us how to fend for ourselves,
catch food, make fire, cook outdoors,
and make warm shelter.

He gave us opportunities
for unique forms of thought patterns,
deeper sorts of problem solving.
The world viewed more clearly.

The world seen through a wider scope
made more real.

Life lived impeccably
in the natural world,
parallel to, but inclusive of,
the confines of life
in a world
we call
"real."

Different Perspectives

One day, he took us to a copse of trees. While sitting under a canopy of newly-formed leaves beneath a clear-blue sky, he showed us a world through different lenses. Perceptions unlike anything we had ever seen or thought we knew. His thoughts about nature different than anything learned before.

Part of a Greater Whole

He showed us how leaves dancing with the wind are not separate forces. Rather, they are joined together. They don't co-exist as separate forces. They **are** one force joined. Part of a bigger picture. A larger whole with awareness stretching outward through the air we breathe, then further into sun's light and beyond, even into outer space.

And we began to **see** the movements and hear the hissing of wind passing through leaves moving in a world of awareness never seen or felt before.

He pointed to the random patterns of leaves within the sounds of motion created by the wind ever changing; rising and falling, shooting 'round and 'round.

Wind and leaves connected, sharing thoughts, making one another who they are. Endless patterns shared from the wind, the leaves, and branches making interconnections.

Tree roots interconnect with other roots. Billions of interconnections above and below ground around the world.

Trees absorb from nature all that we seek to understand.

Connected to the Sun's Rays

They understand the connection with the sun's rays. They absorb all that is real without conscious thought.

He told us how they reach the tendrils of their minds, the roots of their awareness, into earth where they feel the vibrations of the planet. They understand the vibrations as a language of thought. Everywhere, everything vibrates, gathers, then gives back. The air is filled with vibrations of all sorts, but we can't hear them. This is nature's music. Life's music.

Truths About Life

"Trees are such marvelous beings, aren't they?" he said. "They are a supreme creation of life along the continuum of awareness, able to gather all knowledge from earth and sky. One long strip of awareness from where they are rooted to the edge of the horizon and beyond.

"They know the stuff we struggle to understand while we scurry about like ants grabbing pieces of sticks or crumbs of knowledge left over from a picnic, all while thinking how clever we are."

New Morning Light

Watching night birds take nighttime flight,
I walk the line where all three meet,
sky within dark water,
waves of moonlight,
sparkling grains of sand,
reflecting light below/above
within their kisses
of the night.

I looked into the grounds of sweet goodbyes,
thoughts of daylight in disguise,
with each new morning light,
the sky that touches deep inside,
the sound of the inland seas.

Drawn back into the dream, I close my eyes.
With speckled stars above the nighttime breeze,
with moonlight showing through the trees,
I'll sleep and dream 'til morning light
when daylight birds
take morning flight.

Winter

Bluegills

At a farm just outside town, Dad and I buy two cardboard containers packed with fifteen or twenty corn bores covered in loose, black muck.

Five miles later, we turn left onto a gravel road. Fields of snow, differing shades of gray and white, stretch to a line of trees barely discernible in the distance. Snow tornadoes rise and fall, reforming to rise and fall again and again. Snow swirling through the air creates a fog making it hard to distinguish where field and pale gray sky begin and end.

Three miles later, we park next to a mountain of snow plowed higher than the car. A hundred yards beyond the mountain, a frozen inland lake waits for us to spend the rest of the day fishing through holes chopped in the ice.

We drag the plywood fish boxes up and over the snow. A cold Arctic wind blows hard against our backs as we trudge through knee-deep powder snow to the shoreline of the lake.

Cautiously, we shuffle between patches of snow and the smooth, black ice. Occasionally, we hold each other's mittened hand for extra balance. We don't want to take any chances. A slippery fall could cause serious damage to butt bones, kneecaps, and elbows. A cracked skull could ruin a perfectly good day of fishing.

A quarter-mile across the ice not far from the opposite shoreline, Dad chooses a spot where he thinks we can catch some fish.

Next, he chops four eighteen-inch-diameter holes through two-foot-thick ice using a four-foot-long iron bar called a spud. The end that chops through the ice is rounded and flat. A leather strap at the opposite end wraps around Dad's wrist. This keeps the spud from slipping into black water when punched through the last few inches of ice.

Dad works carefully to keep the sidewalls straight. Sidewalls that taper funnel-like to the bottom make the hole smaller. It takes longer to pull a large bluegill through a hole even slightly too small. Bluegills wiggle and twist with a hook in their mouth. Given enough time, they can shake themselves free. It's best to set the hook and pull them out of the water quickly thus denying them the time needed to escape. A funnel-shaped hole makes it impossible to land a bigger fish like a pike!

What a terrible price to pay for being too lazy to keep the sidewalls straight!

For the rest of the day, we move from hole-to-hole scooping films of ice that form almost within seconds over exposed water. Hunched over on our fish boxes, the cold wind flowing aerodynamically over our backs, we stare down at the holes waiting patiently for the slightest movement of our bobbers.

From time to time we check our tip ups, just in case the bait has been stolen.

Tip ups are extra fish lines put at various locations. When a fish takes or nibbles on the bait, a spring-loaded mechanism sets the hook. A red flag tips up.

When the red flag tips up, we quickly drop our ice poles and rush over. I'm the first to get there and retrieve the line in a hand-over-hand fashion. The bluegill flips and flops as it emerges from the black water. After removing the hook, I drop it into the bottom of my fish box with four or five others already frozen stiff.

With the bluegill's soft mouth and gentle pull, I lose more of the plump, white corn bores than fish I catch. Dad catches twice as many. After a lifetime of ice fishing, he can detect the gentle pull of a bluegill and set the hook. Inexperienced as I am, I still manage to pull in ten or twelve before the day is over.

At times, the ice makes fearful sounds. Thundering or moaning menacingly like an angry bear having a nightmare. Powerful ripping sounds heard in the distance suddenly crackle and moan for seconds at a time. Jagged points of iced lightning traveling a great distance suddenly etch close to where we sit, sending shivers of fear through me. But I don't say anything.

While the temperatures stay low, the lake makes ice twenty-four hours a day. New ice expands creating fractures. When a single sheet of ice cracks, it loses its stability. Driven by the force of expanding ice, the surfaces grinding against each other are like the tectonic plates of the earth.

The sound of the growing ice has a powerful, at times almost overwhelming, effect on me. I sit rigidly, preoccupied as a vision repeats itself. A slab of ice breaks. Helplessly, we slide down the slippery surface, swallowed into the jaws of the cold, black depths below where not even the slightest ray of light can possibly escape.

At day's end, the sun becomes a vague halo of yellowish light against a drab sky. With less heat from the sun, a dreary gray sky makes the day seem colder, giving me the chills.

We pack our poles and tip ups into our fish boxes, twenty to thirty bluegills frozen stiff at the bottom. Then we begin our trek back to the car.

Facing downward against the Arctic wind, we shuffle across the slippery surface toward the shoreline. The tips of my fingers and toes are numb. My face burns from the cold wind.

At the shoreline, we pull our fish boxes through a trail blazed by our bodies breaking through thigh-deep powdered snow. Struggling against the Arctic wind, we pull our fish boxes over the mountain of snow to the warmth of the car.

We drive through the dimming light of late afternoon into the dark of midwinter's early night, arriving home just in time for dinner.

Snow

I love when snow falls in big cities
forcing people to stay inside
with their families, significant others,
or self, away from the noise
and forced hustle and bustle
of everyday life.

I love to go outside after snow falls
and see the world coated white.
The forms of life and its manifestations
turned smooth, curved, soft, and so clean!

At night, the snow world sparkles.
Especially during full, half, and quarter moons.
Or from the connection
between sparkling night skies.
Light beams sharing
more than we can imagine.

Snow acoustics are the best!
Inside the silence of freshly-fallen snow,
all distractions melt away
allowing soft sounds of our true selves
to emerge.

Freshly-fallen snow gives back
precious remembrance of time past
when visions and forgotten feelings
are seen anew;
stripped bare of all nonessentials.
Like an epic tale told with few words
or a world seen through a prism
of crystal-clear
ice.

Lake Huron Shoreline
Spring Thaw

Within the Light of Darkest Night

I sit and watch in peaceful trance
Great Lake's water cascade toward me.
Its white caps reaching
for the shore
where purest water and sand
meet in perfect harmony.

A mile offshore, men fish
between shallow water, colored tan,
and deep-water blue extending
to the horizon and beyond.

Suddenly, the world and everything in it comes alive.

An immense delta-shaped cloud, miles across,
morphs into a giant sparrow,
its tail feathers, tendril-like,
emerging from a roiling line of black,
trailing far behind,
each twisting through air,
in its own unique way.

Parts of the whole drifting away,
thin strands of cloud DNA
seeking like-minded life forms,
reforming into new, more powerful forces
or receding into the mist.

92

I listen for words grown silent,
empty spaces greater than
the sound of crashing waves,
or the passing wind that fills my ears
when I find myself surrounded
by shades of gray.

The sandy bottom of the Great Lake
becomes a dark shade of gray
seen strobe-like; the waves,
pale shades with motion.

Streaks of orange
cross the gray sky
from setting sun.

Beach grass slowly darkens
as evening light dims
toward the blue black
of night.

I was living in the gray zone
before nightfall,
on the boundary line
between time.

Where dreams
from beyond the horizon
are born within the light
of darkest
night.

Into the Coldness of My Despair

There's an indentation in the park where there was a clay pit a hundred years ago. The clay was used to make bricks that built the town.

A hundred years later, the clay pit remains as an indentation in the park where each year a volunteer fireman opens a fire hydrant. Water flowing into the indentation makes a nice little skating pond where I skate as often as possible.

The pond is easy to get to. It's only a block and a half from my house along Monroe Road.

I love to ice skate.

Some days I skate from morning until night with a break for lunch. After lunch, it's back to the pond until it's time for dinner. Plenty of times, I skate after dinner when the lights are turned on twice a week.

One day, I lose track of time and skate well into the evening darkness. I don't realize how late it is until I start feeling cold. A jolt of fear courses through me. If I'm not home soon, I'll be guilty of breaking The Cardinal Rule: We don't care what you're doing as long as you are home in time for dinner!

I'm trapped between being **almost** late and **being** late for dinner.

I'm feeling anxious and scared. My only desire is to traverse the one long block and a half between the pond and home. My mind thinks two thoughts: taking a hot shower down in the basement before dinner and how am I going to traverse the block and a half home so I can take a hot shower?

I Have to Take My Skates Off

One way or the other, I have to take my skates off. So I skate over and sit on the park bench.

Taking my gloves off, I discover I've lost most of the feeling in my fingertips making it impossible to unlace my skates.

Not that it matters! The laces on both skates are covered with a thick layer of ice. Even if I could unlace them, I can't imagine exposing my already-frozen fingers **and** feet to the air long enough to pull my boots on.

My mind is blank. The longer I sit, the colder I feel.

Things take a turn for the worse when I realize my options.

The Rise of Nighttime Immensity

As the night sky darkens with its immensity, so do my feelings of coldness and despair.

In frustration, I stand, and while rocking left-to-right, right-to-left, try to picture the fastest way to get home. I keep mumbling, "How am I supposed to walk all the way home with my skates on??"

I ask myself the same question several times. I even ask it out loud, but an answer doesn't come. Finally when the answer comes, I'm so cold and frustrated, I feel like bawling.

I have two choices; walk home with my skates on, or sit on the bench and freeze to death. My parents would hate that. So, I guess there's only one thing left to do.

Resigned to my fate, I do what must be done. Shoving both gloved hands inside my boots, I trudge through calf-deep snow toward the sidewalk wearing my skates. I'm unable to stifle my angry tirades **"Arrrawww! I haaate this!"**

At the sidewalk, I turn right and begin the trek home, my hands, and feet, and face burning from the unrelenting cold.

Dragging Forward/Frozen Snot

Walking a straight line wearing ice skates is nearly impossible. The thin blades can't support the body's weight without forward motion. The slightest movement away from one center of gravity to another causes wobbling. Your skates break outward or inward at an oblique angle. Your ankles drop down assuming the responsibility for sustaining the body's weight while keeping it upright.

The shoe part of my skates are nearly parallel to the sidewalk. One leg cannot support my entire body. So, neither foot can leave the ground. I have to drag each skate forward. The blades scrape over the concrete sounding like knives being sharpened. I slowly drag myself along the sidewalk, one painful step at a time.

My hands are stuffed inside my boots giving me a little extra warmth. I realize how ridiculous I must look with a boot on each hand. I briefly picture myself falling forward leaving tracks in the snow, looking like some four-legged beast with strange-looking front feet and narrow-blade-like back feet. It is funny in a ridiculous way but it passes through my brain like a distant thought not worth thinking about. It lifts my spirits a little.

Next, I find myself thinking how strange it is that the block and a half walk **to** the skating pond took ten or fifteen minutes. With fingers and toes burning, my lip turning stiff for some reason, my eyes watering, feeling frozen to the bone, it seems like on the **return** trip, I'm **miles** from home.

I realize the extra weight I'm carrying on my upper lip is frozen snot. With boots on my hands, it's impossible to wipe the frozen snot away. Not being able to get rid of the layers of frozen snot feels like an itch I can't scratch.

To make matters worse, when my eyes start watering, the top and bottom eyelashes freeze together. I have to blink two or three times to wrench them apart. Between the frozen snot on my lip and my frozen eyelashes, it definitely feels like I've got a couple of itches I can't scratch.

I have to accept the fact that there's nothing I can do about the frozen snot on my upper lip or my frozen eye lashes. I feel myself smiling at a funny thought when I picture what might happen if I were to forget my hands are inside my boots. I might decide to wipe the frozen snot off my upper lip, but instead, I'd kick myself in the forehead. Mom and Dad would want to know why I had a boot print on my forehead.

This would be hard to explain.

If I unconsciously raise my hand too quickly to brush away the ice freezing my eyelashes together, I could knock myself out. I could accidentally kick myself in the nose causing me to bleed all over the white snow.

Shaking my head while squinting, releases my eyes from the frozen tears. A few of the frozen tears melt on my cheek and drip down to my jawline. A couple tears briefly form little icicles.

Despite the pain, I'm relieved to be within striking distance from home. Only one house and an empty lot separate me from the house. I see the porch light. Somebody's probably waiting for me.

"If I'm late, at least they'll know how hard I tried."

Finally, I'm on the property climbing up the bank diagonally, no longer feeling hopeless and depressed. I'm within striking distance of my goal. I'm still cold and hurting, but funny thoughts have tempered my misery. I'm still smiling at the thought of kicking myself in the eye.

Climbing the bank with my skates on isn't so hard. The ankle-deep snow with a little crust on top helps support my ankles. I'm tempted to lean forward using my hands to make boot prints in the snow when—

I feel weightless, whisked away by some external force. By and by, I find myself inside the screened-in porch on the side of the house where the big elm grows. I catch a glimpse of Dad entering the kitchen through the sliding-glass door.

A Hot Shower

Mom uses a spoon to chip the ice away from the laces. Getting the skates off is a long, hard process. Everything is stiff and cold. But eventually, we prevail.

Through the sliding-glass door, we head across the kitchen to the door leading down to the basement where a shower stall in the far corner waits for my presence. A warm oasis in a desert of ice.

Eight steps later, I'm in the basement; the shower stall I dreamed about within reach. Mom helps me unravel myself from the wet layers of clothes.

Suddenly I find myself in the oasis I dreamed about along my cold journey home. Streams of water bombard my head. The water breaks apart forming rivers of warmth. Angling my head,

I guide the warmth to different parts of my body or stand in one place letting the water wrap its warmth around me.

I lose track of time immersed in memories along the trail, amazed at the progression of events. I smile at the funny thoughts I had along the way.

I've learned an important lesson. When you're struggling with something painful, it's best to find something to smile about instead of focusing on the pain! It sure helps pass the time.

By and by, I hear three thuds on the floor from above. It's Dad letting me know I've used up enough hot water. I hate it when he cuts my showers short by stomping on the floor. But it seems his thuds are halfhearted. He has already waited a long time beyond the time he usually allows my brother and me to be in the shower.

But it doesn't matter. I feel colder water slowly replacing the hot. I've used up an entire tank of hot water. I turn the water off and step out. "Gee, thanks, Pops," I hear myself say.

That Night/Next Day

At dinner, I feel so drowsy I can hardly keep my eyes open. In fact, I can't remember even finishing dinner. I voluntarily go to bed well before eight-thirty. I don't remember going upstairs.

I look out at the field and stars. I smile wondering if I'll ever be able to tell the story of dragging my skates a block and a half through the cold, wearing a pair of boots on my hands, with frozen snot on my upper lip, frozen eyelashes, and icicles along my jawline? Still smiling, I think that maybe someday I'll write it all down for others to read about.

Shortly, I feel drowsy. I feel my eyes slowly droop.

The last thought I have before drifting off to sleep is a revelation! *Tomorrow's Sunday! No school! I can go skating all day long!*

I slipped into darkness with a smile still on my face.

A Christmas Story

It's cold and crisp outdoors,
air crystal clear between falling flakes.
Light wings fat with fluff,
sailing where they please,
drifting sideways in the breeze with crystal memories.

See them resting quietly in the trees?
On the ground, adding curve to rugged spaces,
giving shadows warm embraces?
Hear them dampening sound with suspense
and quiet anticipation?

See the ground with sparkling memories
of all the Christmases past?

Each snowflake reflecting back
the light from
its own special star?

Or so, we liked to think.

The Stage is Set

And so, the stage is set for the most memorable Christmas of my life when, as a ten-year-old boy, the entire family (aunts, uncles, cousins, and grandparents) gathered at our house for a rare celebration of gift giving on Christmas Eve when a surprise guest came into our midst adding even more magic to that magical time.

Stranded at the Depot/A Stranger in the Night

This was the year my grandfather, Dusty Peck, who worked at the Grand Trunk Railroad Depot, brought home a guest from Canada stranded at the station with no place to sleep on Christmas Eve after blizzard conditions forced the cancellation of passenger-train service to Chicago. We welcome her into our home as an honored guest.

High Jinks and Hilarity

A stranger in our midst adds an air of excitement to the festivities. Knowing rules will be relaxed in her presence, we give little effort to restrain our laughter and sense of mirth reveling in the joy we create as our Christmas gift to her.

I can still picture her sitting next to the fireplace in the blue Naugahyde chair, her head thrown back, mouth wide open, laughing along with everyone when Uncle Bill lost his balance while bouncing around the living room on a pogo stick, knocked over a lamp, then rolled onto the lamp shade while trying to stand up.

Up in Flames

This is the same year that most of the frilly, girly gifts my two girl cousins received went up in flames after being accidentally gathered together with all the Christmas wrappings and burned in the fireplace.

Everyone is sympathetic while my one cousin cries. My brother and I think it's hilarious!

Roasting

This is also the year that Dad decides we'll have a traditional-style roasted pig with an apple in its mouth for dinner on Christmas Day.

Our oven isn't big enough for a whole pig so a baker named Mr. Gregory, who lives in the apartment above the bakery downtown, gives us permission to use his big gas-fired oven with rotating shelves to slow roast the pig all day.

Parked in the Alley

Shortly after sunrise on Christmas morning with temperatures below freezing, we park in the alley behind the bakery. The back door is unlocked. Ten feet from the back door, we see the wide stainless-steel door of the big oven.

Baker's Hours

Mr. Gregory bakes bread starting at four a.m. every morning. He doesn't mind lighting the gas oven Christmas morning before we arrive. We don't expect what happens next.

When Dad pulls open the stainless-steel door handle, warm, dry, desert-like heat washes over our faces and hands reminding us how cold it is a few feet behind us just outside the back door.

Electric Motor, Chain, BB Holes Along a Metal Tube

A long chain moving over sprockets turned by an electric motor pulls the shelves around blue flames hissing through BB-sized holes along a metal tube the width of the oven.

Our pig rests on a square, cast iron skillet with curled edges so that juice won't leak inside Mr. Gregory's oven **and** to capture the juice that my grandmother will use to make her delicious ham gravy.

We tent the pig with an extra-heavy strip of aluminum foil folded down the middle. Dad uses a wooden baker's pole to slide the cast iron skillet into the center, close, but not too close, to the blue flames.

Before leaving we turn the motor on, pull the back door tightly shut, and drive home.

Every two or three hours during the day, we drive downtown to the bakery to check on the progress of our roasting pig. The blue gas flames light the inside of the oven just enough for us to see it turning golden brown as it slowly rolls past our eyes.

Later That Afternoon/A Pig in a Blanket

Later that afternoon around five o'clock, the pig is cooked to a dark, rich, golden color. It doesn't need to be roasted any longer. We use the baker's pole to pull the big skillet to the edge of the open door where we cover it with more aluminum foil.

Wearing thick insulated gloves, we lift the pig and iron skillet from the oven, and carry it down the back steps to the car where we place it covered with more foil into the trunk of the car with blankets over the top. While Dad warms up the car, I run back inside to close the oven door and make sure the back door is slammed tightly shut!

On the way home, we laugh about having a pig in a blanket in the trunk of the car.

Dining

We need two dining tables to comfortably seat ten people; one aunt, one uncle, two girl cousins, a grandmother, a grandfather, a brother, Mom and Dad, and our guest from Canada.

The menu includes scalloped corn, scalloped oysters, and fresh green beans, onions, and bacon sautéed in bacon fat tossed with apple cider vinegar and a touch of sugar.

Dad carves the meat into chunks that are so tender they fall apart when served. A combination of flavors; cloves and cinnamon and garlic and onion fill the air. I finally understand what melts in your mouth means! My grandmother's ham gravy forms golden pools on top of Mom's creamy-smooth mashed potatoes.

Grandpa eats mint jelly with venison Dad set aside as a special treat. My cousins, my brother, and I drink tall glasses of milk. My grandparents drink black coffee with their meal while the adults drink red wine.

For dessert, there's apple and pecan pie, my favorite. Each year, Dad makes a creamy rich sauce in a double boiler from butter, sugar, and an egg yolk that makes even fruitcake taste good! Everyone raves about Grandma Peck's apple pie, and we all get a good laugh when she tells us it is "mock apple pie" made with Ritz Crackers!

Telling Stories

The adults keep us entertained with funny or interesting stories about growing up or daily life.

We relive Uncle Bill's accident with the pogo stick. Each of us tells what we saw from different points of view. Each story is a different version, but they're all the same, and we laugh a little harder with each re-telling.

My brother said it looked like Uncle Bill was shot from a cannon when he flew into the table knocking over the lamp.

The lady from Canada tells us her sister lives in Chicago where she works as a bookkeeper at the Chicago stockyards. Our guest lives in Thunder Bay, Ontario, where she books fishing expeditions into the Canadian bush country on the Alcona Railroad.

At the County Fair 1918

Grandma and Grandpa tell how they met at the Shiawassee County Fair during a band concert in 1918. Grandma tells how hard they worked growing up on farm ten or fifteen miles outside of Owosso tending the big family garden, canning fruits and vegetables all summer long, stocking up for cold winters, caring for the farm animals seven days a week, gathering hay before hay balers, or harvesting corn with implements that seem ancient today. There was no electricity or indoor plumbing. Despite what we think of as hardships, Grandma Peck said she had a wonderful childhood growing up on a farm out in the country with lots of brothers and sisters.

Tap Dancing on the Radio

Mom and Aunt Jo talk about the beautiful costumes Grandma made for them when they tap danced at gatherings in different towns and cities all around the state.

They re-live their experience riding the train to Chicago where, since television hadn't been invented, they tap danced on a popular radio program!

Mom and Aunt Jo

The Episodic Past

I have many boyhood memories from Christmases past, but they are all episodic. Scattered memories from different years. There was the Christmas Eve Dad and I rode around town leaving turkeys on the doorsteps of families not as fortunate as ours.

There's a partial memory I have of a boy walking down the aisle at the Congregational Church cradling his favorite gift: a white football that I left at the altar for some less fortunate boy.

Then there's the year I got the second-best gift ever (the first being a new bicycle), a new pair of black figure skates with runners that, as Dad pointed out, were made of Sheffield steel.

Ice Skating in Winter Wonderland

Very early that Christmas morning after the gifts are opened, the sun barely casting a gray shadow onto the world, I grab my new skates, sneak out the side door, cross the road, walk west a block and a half along the north side of the athletic field to the ice pond in the park where I skate in a magical world devoid of human movement or sound. It feels like I'm dancing with an invisible partner carving out figure eights any size I want, free to skate as fast as I want, then turn and use the sharp teeth at the front of my blades to cut curved grooves in the solid ice showering fractured ice crystals curling to the sides like broken waves while stopping on a dime.

Other Stories

All the Christmas memories are special. But nothing compares to the year we celebrated Christmas on Christmas Eve when the Canadian lady became part of our family making our Christmas celebration even more special. Especially since all the inns in town were closed. It almost seems like she was meant to be with us. Her presence was a gift releasing a spark that added extra measures of laughter and joy. By her presence, we were elevated into becoming the best people we could be, even *more* full of love and giving.

By the time our guest departed the next day, she had become a special part of our lives. She will **always** be a part of who I am. A vivid memory from beginning to end.

Where I'll Sleep

I want to be buried surrounded
by the fields of my youth,
next to other kindred souls
who decided to lie in similar peace
on that grassy knoll, sheltered by a giant oak,
its limbs spread wide to shield us,
its roots embracing our boxed homes,
cradling us in our sleep.

Distant from the hub-bub of life,
too far away for casual visitors
with plastic flowers.

Our serenity only slightly disturbed
by the occasional car rushing past.
The sound of tires rolling fast,
metal barreling through thick air
rising from summer heat
when corn silk and yellow seedlings,
trees and grass, all join in the dance of life,
thrusting higher and higher toward the sun,
the same as my neighbors when they produced seed,
multiplied, then passed on
leaving tiny bits of themselves behind
to prove there's life after.

In the stillness of winter's coldest clear night,
I'll rise from within the earth to glide on moon's rays;
the wind my flesh, the air my breath, the stars my sight,
the oak tree above my haven.

At the End of the Day

Shedding Light on Poetry

Rhyme, Breaks, Punctuation, Creation, Humor

I write prose and poetry, but consider myself a poet first because most of my prose is born from the poetic process.

I believe poets must discover their own individual and unique form, format, voice, and style. I'd like to share with you the thoughts I have about my poetry and prose that may shed some light on my writing.

Rhyme is not requisite with my poetry, but when I hear it alongside the words I'm struggling to choose from, it's always a pleasant surprise. I strive to make rhymes happen if I can. I use my rhyme with a sense of onamonapia and pacing. I will purposely break a line to create rhyme because it tends to push the poem along with sound.

Breaks are important to me because they encapsulate thoughts and visions. Breaks can be seen as a moment the writer gives the reader time to allow them to clarify their thinking before moving on to the next point. Breaks are rest stops along the pathway that guide the reader toward resolution at the end.

My line breaks and words at the end of lines are intentional efforts meant to draw the reader to the edge of the next thought. I break lines where I find keywords, generating a sense of curiosity about what's next. I want the reader to fall over the edge of each line, drawn downward by curiosity, seeking completion of incomplete thoughts or incomplete thoughts seeking completion, additional clues that lead to meaning or visual details inside worlds created.

I arrange the lines of my stanzas across the middle of the page like vocalizations on graph paper. I seek resolution at the end of each stanza using a single word pointing down the page to the next stanza, the next perspective, the next new place, a final unexpected thought, and the grain of truth readers expect at the end of a poem.

The Oak Trees in Florida
One day, walking
beside a freshwater stream,
I watch individual water bugs disappear
from a group of twenty or thirty
gathered in the shadow of weeds
along the creek bank, devoured
by some small fish
I could not see.

Lousy endings leave me feeling flat, disillusioned, suspended, wondering, confused, unsatisfied, even resentful.

I like to give an unexpected sense of surprise somewhere along the comedy/tragedy spectrum. Humor and tragedy both share a powerful force resulting in unexpected surprise.

Humor is a great form of resolution. I try to use unexpected events, words, or idiotic scenes causing laughter and humorous insight after sudden unexpected discoveries.

How I Do It

I start by throwing down words and phrases that come to me, like clay thrown onto a potter's wheel or a block of marble to be sculpted.

After moving things around, certain words or phrases create a flash of light, and momentarily, I might find a spark of meaning. It could be something colorful and thought-provoking, or fragmented and abstract, or worthless to pursue, like discovering you're on the wrong path to the Emerald City.

When I find something with viable meaning or even a single word, I start to work as a sculptor with a slab of marble searching for the forms hidden inside. For me, it's the search for form within the words thrown down.

I like to build my words with sound and color, definition and beat. All are equally important to me. It seems poetry and narrative can be abstract and meander but behind whatever form it takes, there needs to be a good rhythm section.

Sometimes when I'm really lucky I can play the words like Thelonius Monk!

At other times I wax poetic in storytelling mode, happy if it's even a fraction as good as Stephen Vincent Benet, my favorite poet/storyteller. Now I'm working on a jigsaw puzzle with a paint brush adding details or erasing, sometimes endlessly. Faces and shit emerge from the fog.

I try to write in reference to, or one step removed from, the obvious. Why should I make it easy for the reader to understand the meaning? Meaning is to be searched for. Meaning isn't easy to find because it doesn't exist on the surface. Beauty exists on the surface and so does meaning but in a different way. Meaning twists and swirls throughout the work of an artist, unseen but seen. Meaning enhances beauty as does light.

Meaning is sensed and felt. Most often, meaning is a mystery. It seems sophomoric and dull to **not** have to search for meaning. What is the use in being concrete and oversimplified if it doesn't arouse a sense of wonder or a sense of freedom?

Real meaning elicits different thoughts and perspectives from each viewer/reader. Or the feeling of being transported through space and time.

I let the abstract carry me along. Often it feels like I'm channeling from some source of creativity below the surface. I don't know the place. All I can say is that it's a river of creativity and it has to do with dreams. Occasionally the river floods its banks and we glimpse a different world beyond the so-called real world.

As I struggle to make sense of my words, I start seeing events from the past. When light sparks for fractions of a second, I might see exchanges between myself and people or circumstances I hadn't thought about for years: catching a grounder at first base, bedroom scenes, the time I met a friend on the street I hadn't seen for years, or the hilarity my best friend and I felt walking home from school when we heard the word "bullshit" spoken for the first time.

Mine is a visual world formed by words used as blocks to build visions of place and time. The meaning of my work is the clarity of place and time within the reality of the narrative. Place and time and life conjured up from time gone past giving life meaning in the present. Reminders of the world we came from.

I keep working, dabbing some purple there, striking long lines for simplicity. This goes on and on until I feel I've found and formed something from the words and should step away. If I don't, I often spoil the freshness even though the words might not be grammatically correct.

Too many distractions blow a hole through the finality of a pretty good ending.

Or maybe I'll go back and throw it in the trash.

About the Author

I grew up in Durand, Michigan, population 4,500, the railroad center of the state, during a fifteen year window of time I call the Golden Age of America 1950–1965. Summers at the family cottage along the northern shoreline of Lake Huron on Tawas Point are the inspiration for most of my stories.

In 1965, I graduated from the same high school as my parents, one grandfather, and a great aunt attended during the early 1900s. After high school, I attended Eastern Michigan University in Ypsilanti, Michigan, where I received my B.S. Degree in psychology with a minor in literature in 1969.

From 1969–1970, I taught third grade at the same elementary school I attended as a boy alongside teachers I had growing up.

After teaching, I spent a year in grad school, before migrating to Tarpon Springs, Florida. In 1976, I moved to New York City where I became a Placement Specialist with Enwood Personnel, 6 East 45th Street, not far from the United Nations.

I married my first wife, Suzanne, in 1976. We had one child, our daughter Laura Beth, in New York before moving to Port Charlotte, Florida in 1979. Our son, John Adam was born in 1980.

I've been married to Jodi for thirty-five years. Together we have four grown kids, four grandchildren, an angelic daughter-in-law, and two incredible sons-in-law. Retired now, we travel between our home in Port Charlotte, Florida, a cottage in Tawas, Michigan, Atlanta, Georgia, Seattle, Washington, and all points in between.

1950schildhood.wordpress.com   *FathomPublishing.com*